You Can
Change Your
Whole Life

TITLES BY JOSEPH MURPHY

AVAILABLE IN PRINT AND EBOOK FROM G&D MEDIA

This Is It

How to Use Your Healing Power

Living Without Strain

Love is Freedom

Magic of Faith

Peace Within Yourself

Pray Your Way Through It

Prayer is the Answer

Quiet Moments with God

Techniques in Prayer Therapy

The Miracles of Your Mind

Traveling with God

You Can Change Your Whole Life

AVAILABLE IN EBOOK FROM G&D MEDIA

Believe in Yourself

Fear Not

How to Attract Money

How to Use the Power of Prayer

Nuclear Religion

Riches Are Your Right

Stay Young Forever

The Healing Power of Love

The Meaning of Reincarnation

Why Did This Happen to Me?

You Can Change Your Whole Life

Joseph Murphy
Ph.D., D.D.

MEDIA

Contents

1   Banish That Feeling of Guilt   7

2   Your Will and God's Will   31

3   The Love That Casts Out Fear   45

4   Removing Mental Stumbling Blocks   63

5   To Be, to Do, and to Have   77

6   The Mysteries and Wonders of Sleep   89

7   Not Resigned, but Reconciled   103

8   The Master Secret of the Ages   117

9   You Are What You Eat   129

10   The Magic Quality of Self-confidence   147

11   The Master Key to Harmonious
Human Relations   161

About the Author   177

1

Banish That Feeling Of Guilt

But if the wicked will turn from all his sins that he hath committed, and keep all my statutes, and do that which is lawful and right, he shall surely live, he shall not die. All his transgressions that he hath committed, they shall not be mentioned unto him: in his righteousness that he hath done he shall live.

EZEKIEL 19:21–22.

The wicked are the bewitched and means anyone who thinks negatively and destructively. Life holds no grudge against any living being in the world. God is Life, and this Life-Principle is moving in you now animating, sustaining, and strengthening you. If you are wondering where God is, the Life-Principle in you is God. You are alive with the life of God.

Life is forever forgiving us. We must let the scales of superstition fall from our eyes and become aware of simple truths which were always known. Truth has been distorted, twisted, and prostituted beyond recognition. This is why guilt is universal. In all ages people have been told to banish this sense of guilt, and they employed various ceremonies and rituals for this purpose. In olden days they sacrificed their bullocks and doves to propitiate the gods of wrath. When storms came, crops ruined, or a great drought prevailed, the people believed the gods were angry. The jungle priest had to give the people an answer. If he did not give the people an explanation, they killed him. Therefore, the jungle priests gave answers which satisfied the superstitious imaginings of these people.

In remote parts of the world, people have sacrificed their children to appease the so-called angry gods of flood, fire, and famine. This is somewhat like paying a gangster, giving him tribute every week so he will not throw a bomb into your store in order to curry favor with him.

If you burn your hand, life forgives you, reducing the edema, giving you new skin, tissue, and cells. Life does not hold a grudge against you. If you injure your hand, cutting it severely, life forgives you. New cells build bridges over the cut. Life is always forgiving you. Life is givingness and forgiveness. If you take some bad food, life forgives you, too, and causes you to expel and regurgitate it. Life has no ill-will against you.

We must learn to use the Life-Principle the right way and cease going against the stream of life. When a child is born, it is Universal Life individualizing Itself and appearing in your home; rejoice! The child has no discrimination nor discernment; it has not begun to use its reason as yet; therefore it is subject to the mood of parents. Every child wants to follow its own inner inherent drives, and it thinks nothing evil about these things, but the father or mother who does not understand says, "You little brat, you are a sinner. You are a naughty boy. God is going to punish you. You are going to suffer for this." The child is baffled; he cannot reason out what is wrong as he lacks discernment. He, therefore, feels cut off from love, protection, and security for that is what the mother represents to him. He feels that his mother is angry, and he reacts perhaps by micturating at night, indicating the child wants to drown his mother in resentment. The child may also react in this way by becoming timid, weak, and inferior, showing a deep sense of rejection.

A young boy might react to a cruel tyrannical father by becoming hostile, belligerent, and resentful. He knows his father is a big man, so he suppresses his anger. His rage is suppressed and it becomes a festering sore. Later on he finds himself opposed to authority because he has been against his father all his young life. He gets in trouble with the policeman, the professor at school, and other symbols of authority. He is always fighting his father, and he does not know it because no one has ever taught him how his mind works.

The President of the United States is subject to authority. Congress has power over him. We have to live and adjust to authority. Wherever we go, there is authority. We must learn to establish control over our thoughts, feelings, and responses. We must take charge of our own minds. When we do take charge of this motley crew in our minds and say to them, "I am the master, I am going to order my thoughts around and tell them what to give attention to," we will be like an employer ordering his employees to execute his instructions.

Man must take charge of his own mind and not permit others to govern it for him. Creed, dogma, tradition, superstition, fear, and ignorance rule the mind of the average man. The average man does not own his own mind. It does not belong to him. It is often ruled over and governed by the rank superstitions of others.

We must realize that a great sense of guilt comes from what is called conscience. A great number of people think that the voice of conscience is that of God. It is not. Conscience is your inner feeling and the voice of someone else. Often it is the voice of fear, superstition, and weird concepts of God. I knew a boy who feared that he would be punished by God because he did not go to church on Sunday. This is the inner voice of superstition and false belief implanted in his subconscious by his parents or teachers. This belief on the part of the boy gave him a sense of guilt, and he felt that he must be punished.

When you were young, you were given taboos, restrictions, homilies, and a series of don'ts. You were perhaps told that you were evil, a sinner, and that God would punish you. Perhaps you were told of a lake of fire waiting for you, if you did not behave and believe in a particular creed. The minds of children are contaminated and polluted with all kinds of strange notions and false doctrines.

A young boy said to me, "If I ride my bicycle without lights, I would feel that I must be punished, that I must fall because my mother said, 'You will fall. You are going to be hurt. You are naughty. You are going to be punished.'"

What a disastrous thing to tell a child. It would be so much better to tell him that he should not ride a bicycle at night without lights. Mother and father should explain thoroughly to the boy that the instructions are for his own good, for his own self-preservation. It is much better to tell a boy that God's Love will always take care of him rather than frighten him with dreadful, hypnotic suggestions of danger.

Children should never be told that they were born in iniquity and conceived in sin. They should be taught that they are children of God, that God is their real Father, and that God is Love. They also should be taught that Love cannot do anything unloving. Of course, there is the good conscience where the boy is taught the Golden Rule, love of others, and that honesty is the best policy. When a boy is about to steal, there is that within him which tells him, "No, you shouldn't do that."

The mother and father are there to teach the child the difference between rat poison and butter, the difference between the skunk and the cat, the difference between what is right and what is wrong. The child has to go to school. He must learn manners; be indoctrinated properly. He learns what is right, true, noble, and God-like. Yet how many are taught these qualities today?

Everyone wants self-esteem, wants to feel worthy, wants to be recognized by his neighbors as honest, sincere, and good. You want your children and your wife to love you. You want the respect of the community. When a man falls short of expressing himself in doing the right thing, he feels a sense of guilt and proceeds to punish himself.

I knew a man who worked every night until about one o'clock in the morning. He paid no attention to his two boys or his wife. He was always too busy working hard. He thought people should pat him on the back because he was working so arduously and persistently past midnight every night. He had a blood pressure of over two hundred and was full of guilt. Unconsciously, he proceeded to punish himself by hard work and completely ignored his children. A normal man does not do that. He is interested in his boys, etc. He does not shut his wife out of his world.

I explained to him why he was working so arduously, "There is something eating you inside, otherwise, you would not act that way. You are punishing yourself." He did have a sense of guilt. It was toward a brother. Then he realized what he had been doing to himself.

I explained to him that God was not punishing him. If we misused the laws of life, we would suffer accordingly. If a man puts his hand on a naked wire, he will get burned. Electricity itself is not evil. The only sin is ignorance of the law, and the only punishment is the automatic reaction of man's misuse of the law.

If a man misuses the principle of chemistry, he may blow up the office or the factory. If he strikes his hand on a board, he may cause his hand to bleed. The board is not for that purpose. Its purpose may be to lean upon or to support your feet.

This man realized that God does not condemn or punish anyone, and that all his suffering was due to the reaction of his subconscious mind and to his own negative and destructive thinking. He had cheated his brother at one time, and the brother had now passed on. Still he was full of remorse and guilt.

I asked him, "Would you do that now?"

He said, "No."

"You felt that it was the right thing to do at that time?"

His reply was, "Yes."

"But you would not do it now?"

He added, "No. I am helping others to know how to live."

I added the following comment, "You have a greater reason and understanding now. The past is dead, nothing lives but this moment. As you change this moment, you change your destiny. Forgiveness is to forgive yourself. You cannot forgive another without first forgiving yourself. Forgiveness is getting your thoughts in line with the Divine Presence and the Divine Law of Harmony. Self-condemnation is hell, forgiveness is heaven." This man was completely healed and became free.

Self-condemnation is one of the most destructive of all mental poisons sending psychic pus all over your system. It destroys your vitality, enthusiasm, energy, and may affect all the organs of your body.

If you have a glass of dirty water, you may condemn, resent, and curse it indefinitely, but you will not get clean water. However, if you continually pour clean water into the glass, you will have clean water.

A man who murdered his brother in Europe came to see me in Los Angeles some years ago. He was suffering from great mental anguish and torture believing that God must punish him. He explained that his brother was having an affair with his wife and that he shot him on the spur of the moment. This had happened about fifteen years ago. In the meantime, this man had married an American girl and had three lovely children. He was in a position where he helped many people and was a transformed man.

My explanation to him was to the point that physically and psychologically he was not the same man who shot his brother, as they say every cell of our bodies changes every year. Moreover, mentally and spiritually he was a new man. He was full of love and goodwill for humanity. The old man who committed the crime was dead and gone. Actually he was condemning an innocent man!

This man understood and realized that death and resurrection are constantly taking place in our lives.

Man must die to that which he is before he can live to that which he wants to be. This man realized the significance of the following Truths in the Bible: *Come now, and let us reason together, saith the Lord; though your sins shall be as scarlet, they shall be as white as snow; though they be red like crimson, they shall be as wool.* Isaiah 1:18. *And their sins and iniquities will I remember no more.* Hebrews 10:17. *I, even I, am he that blotteth out thy transgressions for mine own sake, and will not remember thy sins.* Isaiah 43:25. *Behold, I make all things new.* Rev. 21:5. *And the Spirit of the Lord will come upon thee, and thou . . . shalt be turned into another man.* I. Samuel 10:6.

Let us suppose that a man misused the law of his mind for fifty years. By trial and error and study he learns how to use his mind by giving constructive imagery, life-giving patterns, and God-like ideas to his subconscious mind. This process would be analogous to pure water flowing into dirty water. By filling his mind with the Truths of God, he would be giving life-giving thoughts to his deeper mind. Then the past mistakes are changed, wiped out, obliterated, and remembered no more.

Begin with God and you end with God. Begin with Love and you end with Love. A new beginning is a new end. Begin now to use your subconscious the right way, and you will no longer experience the negations of the past because the subconscious is changed through prayer. The Healing Presence of God is within you. Let it flow through you and become a channel for His Love, Truth, and Beauty.

To teach children that they are born with the stain of original sin, because Adam and Eve sinned is ecclesiastical verbiage and out of place altogether in the modern interpretation of the Bible. Original sin really means that man has forgotten his Divine Origin and takes the commandments and superstitions of men for the Truths of God. Every child in the world is born into the race mind and all that his environment represents—that is also one of the meanings of original sin.

When you learn the laws of your mind, and your own divinity, you are no longer subject to the taboos, restrictions, false beliefs, and the corrupt indoctrination you received in your youth. If you want to cleanse your children's minds, practice the Presence of God in the home. Think God-like thoughts, then the home will be saturated with a lovely mood or atmosphere. You will see the child grow in the image and likeness of the dominant mood of the home. This is the real meaning of baptism.

Jesus said to the woman caught in adultery, "Woman, where are thine accusers? hath no man condemned thee? Neither do I condemn thee; go, and sin no more."

Truth does not condemn. When we cease accusing ourselves, we are free. God has always forgiven man, but man must forgive himself. Cease mentally stoning and flagellating yourself. Focus your attention on your ideal and with faith in God move forward in the Light.

I will restore to you the years that the locust hath eaten.

The locust represents grief or some other negative state of mind which irritates and annoys you inside. The negative emotion is called the meal of the locust.

Many people are full of guilt because they failed to visit their father or mother prior to their transition to the next dimension. Their statements are somewhat as follows: "Oh, I mistreated my mother before she passed on." "My husband died, and I was out at the time." "I did not forgive my father, and now he is dead and gone." "Etc."

The Bible gives you the answer and teaches you how to forgive yourself and others. The first thing you must realize is that there is no time or space in the Mind-Principle. This very moment you can relax mentally and think of your mother whom you believe you wronged in some way. Imagine that you are talking to her, tell her how lovely and beautiful she is and how much you love her. Exalt her in your mind and realize the Presence of God is there and that His Love, Light,

Truth, and Beauty are flowing through her. Realize also that she is alive with the Life of God. Live in this imaginary scene until you get the fragrant reaction which fills your soul with joy. Continue to dramatize this mental scene, and the reaction will come, and you will feel free; your mother also will be free. The action of God has taken place, your mother will forget all about the incident, and so will you. A complete healing will follow this procedure.

If you made a recording of your talk on a tape machine, you could erase it. In the same manner you can erase these psychic traumas from your subconscious mind by impressing on your subconscious the spiritual truths of God. The new vibratory tone of your thoughts erase the old negative patterns of thought lodged in your subconscious.

A man said to me recently, "My conscience is my guide." He was writing vitriolic articles attacking a certain religious group. I explained to him the working of his deeper mind. He realized that his biases, hatreds, and superstitious patterns were planted in his subconscious mind when he was young and that his mental conditioning was the reason for his resentment, hostility, and antagonism to other religious groups.

Many people have become victims of ruthless superstition and ignorant biases. Following the voice of conscience has ruined the lives of many people. One man I knew said, "I hear a voice inside me urging me to kill my mother-in-law." The voice he heard was real enough, like the voices and scenes you hear in your dreams. The subconscious mind is always dramatizing the impressions we make upon it. It is our Book of Life which keeps a record of all our thoughts, feelings, and beliefs. I explained to him that his constant hatred and resentment of his mother-in-law was murder in his own heart and that his evil and destructive thoughts were constantly sinking down into his mind and would eventually saturate the subconscious with the idea of murder. The subconscious acts by reacting, and the law of the subconscious is one of compulsion; therefore, he would eventually commit the murder. The voices he heard were those of his own subconscious talking back to him. My explanation was the cure. He blessed and prayed for his mother-in-law; they became good friends, and she calls him "my son."

Those who put thousands of Protestants to death in the days of the Spanish Inquisition did so in the name of conscience. This conscience represented religious hatred and bigotry. Research scholars and archaeologists have definite evidence that parents in ancient Babylon stoned children to death because of some minor infraction of certain laws and rules which they promulgated.

Many people walking the streets of Los Angeles are victims of a neurotic conscience. The patterns of conscience vary with different religions, racial and social influences. You must learn to differentiate between what you call conscience and the voice of God. God always speaks in peace and never in confusion. The voice of God is always constructive, harmonious, and peaceful. The voice and intimations of the Divine are always lifeward, tending toward the life more abundant. Whenever you have an urge to go against the laws of life such as the Golden Rule, the Ten Commandments, or Paul's Love Epistle in the thirteenth chapter of Corinthians, you know very well it cannot be the voice of Truth or God.

Some time ago I talked to a young lady aged twenty-two. She was taught it was a sin to dance, to play cards, to swim, and to go out with men. She was threatened by her mother who told her she would burn eternally in hell-fire if she disobeyed her will and her religious teachings. This girl wore a black dress, black stockings. She wore no rouge, lip-stick, or any form of make-up because her mother said that these things were sinful. Her mother told her that all men were evil and that sex was of the devil, simply diabolic debauchery.

This girl was full of guilt. When she went out with young men in the office where she worked, she had a deep sense of guilt and thought that God would punish her. Several eligible young men proposed to her but she said to me, "It is wrong to marry. Sex is evil and I am evil." This was her conscience or early conditioning speaking. Actually it was not her own feeling but the voice of her mother lodged in her sub-conscious depths.

She came to me once weekly for about ten weeks, and I taught her the workings of the conscious and subconscious mind. I gave her my book *The Miracles of Your Mind* and also *Love Is Freedom* which deals with marriage and divorce. She studied these books care-fully and systematically. This young girl realized that she had been completely brain-washed, mesmerized, and conditioned by an ignorant, superstitious, bigoted, and frustrated mother. She broke away completely from her family and started to live a wonderful life.

At my suggestion she dressed up, had her hair attended to. She took lessons in driving from a *man*, and she also took dancing lessons. She learned to swim, play cards, and had a number of dates. She began to love life. She prayed for a divine companion by claiming that Infinite Spirit would attract to her a man who harmonized with her thoroughly. This came to pass. As she left my office one Monday eve-ning, there was a man waiting to see me and I casually introduced them, which is something I rarely do in my office. She said to me on leaving, "I saw that man in my dreams; I know we will get married," and they did. They harmonize with each other perfectly.

My experience with people of all religious persuasions is that conscience, as it is usually found, has been the curse of curses in thousands of lives. What about your conscience? Do you think it is a sin to smoke, to take a glass of wine, to dance, or to go to the movies? Do you think it is a sin to laugh and enjoy yourself? If so, you are very sick psychologically and are a victim of brainwashing. The young child is indoctrinated with father's and mother's ideas and in addition perhaps the weird and superstitious concepts of uncles and aunts, teachers and others who do not always instill and inculcate the Truths of God.

It is shocking and diabolical to inculcate into the minds of children that there is a hell-fire waiting for them if they sin, that there is a devil tempting them, that God will punish them, and that they are here to suffer. It is no wonder that the offices of psychiatrists are full of so-called religious people.

A young girl came to see me stating that she had to wash her hands about one hundred times a day and that she was always afraid of some infection. This girl was a Catholic and her husband was of the Jewish faith. They were quite happy together until she began receiving letters from her mother that she had done great evil and added religious threats plus moral condemnation. I explained to this girl that Love knows no creed, race, or sectarian group. Love transcends all creeds. Furthermore, she realized that no one could break up her marriage when Love reigned supreme. She learned to laugh at herself for being so upset. She understood why her mother wrote these foolish letters. She realized that her mother was brain-washed with religious taboos, prejudices, and strictures of all kinds, and that she was writing from the standpoint of superstition, bias, and ignorance, and not from the standpoint of God or Truth. In God there is no Greek or Jew, no bond or free, no Catholic or Protestant, Hindu or atheist. God has no religion and knows nothing about creeds, dogmas, and man-made opinions. This young lady learned to pray and imagined that she had a letter from her mother which was full of love, kindness, and good will.

I told her the story of Orage, a disciple of Ouspensky, who taught his students as follows: "Compose a letter written as from your friend to yourself which would completely satisfy you if you received it. Put into exact words what you would like your friend to write or say to you."

Every night she would embrace her mother in her imagination and radiate love, peace, and joy to her, and then she would read the imaginary letter from her mother which filled her soul with joy. She continued to do this for about three weeks every night, and at the end of that time, she received a letter from her mother apologizing for her previous letters and containing almost the exact words which she had been picturing, feeling, and rejoicing in each night.

In many parts of the world men have several wives; this is their religious custom or tradition. Our Bible teaches that love is an at-one-ment or a union of two souls seeking their way back to the heart of reality. If an American or Englishman had several wives, his conscience might destroy him because of his sense of guilt. A woman in this country would not want to be one of several wives; she would feel guilty and probably get seriously ill mentally and physically.

Howbeit in vain do they worship me, teaching for doctrines the commandments of men. For laying aside the commandment of God, ye hold the traditions of men . . .

In these few verses tersely put, we have the answer to the guilt complexes of millions of supposedly religious and intelligent people. Do the dead thoughts and doctrinal wrappings and trappings of your parents and grandparents rule and govern you, or are you controlled by God and His Spiritual Truths? Learn the great Law of Life. God is Life, and this Life seeks expression through you as beauty, harmony,

joy, love, order, rhythm, and abundance. The King-
dom of God is within you. Infinite Intelligence will
lead and guide you in all your ways when you turn to
It and call upon It.

You can be inspired from On High by claiming
that "God thinks, speaks, and acts through me now,
and I feel the influx of the Holy Spirit animating and
sustaining me in all my ways." Life cannot wish death.
God is Love, and Love cannot wish anything unloving. God is Peace, and Peace cannot wish pain. The
will of God for you is always something wonderful,
magnificent, and glorious. It is something transcending your fondest dreams. Life feels Itself to be beauty,
joy, peace, love, wisdom, intelligence, and harmony. It
seeks to express all these qualities through you. These
are the murmurings and whisperings of your heart-
strings. This is the true voice of conscience which
urges you to rise higher, to move to higher levels of
awareness.

The Center of Divine Inspiration which inspired
the illumined seers who wrote the Bible, speaks
through the great poets, artists, and writers, and it is
within you and can be contacted at the Divine Center
in your own mind. Your conscience should be guided
by the great Truths of God, the spiritual values of
life by an understanding of the principles and laws
of life. Get acquainted with the Indwelling Presence.

Acquaint now thyself with Him, and be at peace, therefore good shall come unto thee.

It was the voice of conscience which caused the people two thousand years ago to say to Jesus that he should not heal on the Sabbath. These thoughts, traditional beliefs are contrary to the laws of life and are definitely evil and destructive. Do you say to your children: "Your parents have the only truth, you must believe what we say. You must never think for yourself. You must accept our dogma." This is disastrous and utterly dictatorial and a totalitarian attitude. It may well be the case that everything you are teaching them is a lie, and they will grow up so conditioned that when they violate any of these foolish and grotesque taboos which you gave them, they will have a guilt complex and be seized with fear, and then proceed to punish themselves.

The morals of people vary throughout the world and are of a geographical nature. These are based on the mores and traditional concepts of the particular country or race. The moral standards of the various cultures are true only when they conform to the Principle of Life which is forever seeking to express Itself through us as harmony, health, peace, joy, love, symmetry, and the life more abundant.

There are women and men who live in hatred of one another and who are hopelessly incompatible because they are afraid to get a divorce due to religious beliefs. They are full of guilt and believe that God would punish them. They are victims of early training and superstitious dogma implanted in their minds by the bigoted propensities of parents and others. They would rather live the lie than have the decency to break up the lie. They say, "Whom God hath joined together, let no man put asunder." God is Love, and if the heart is the chamber of God's Presence and if Love does not unite the two hearts of the man and woman, the marriage is a mockery, a farce, a sham, and a masquerade.

Many people are full of guilt because they accept as right that which is actually wrong. God condemns no one. God has already forgiven you. Forgive yourself. Change your thought and keep it changed. Think on whatsoever things are true, just, lovely, noble, and of good report. Think from the standpoint of the Golden Rule and the Law of Love. Would you think of disobeying the principles of chemistry, physics, mathematics, and engineering? Would you build a wheel off center? Are you believing in antiquated, dead, grotesque, ignorant superstitions and prejudices in the name of religious beliefs, or have you made a serious inquiry into the workings of your subconscious and conscious mind? The modern scientist has to conform to natural law; he cannot change it. Your religion must also conform to natural law. The result is con-science *with knowing.* The Law of Life is the law of health, happiness, peace, order, beauty, right action, and abundance. Divine Order is Heaven's First Law.

Remember ye not the former things, neither consider the things of old. Isaiah 43:18.

Forgetting those things which are behind, and reaching forth unto those things which are before, press toward the mark for the prize. Phillippians 3:13–14. And enter into the glorious liberty of the sons of God.

2

Your Will and God's Will

Nevertheless, not my will, but thy will be done.

Is this resignation or blind fatalism? It is not! Every man wants to experience God's will because God's will for him is always something wonderful, glorious, magnificent, and joyous.

. . . And his name shall be called Wonderful, Counsellor, The Mighty God, The Everlasting Father, The Prince of Peace. Isaiah 9:6.

The name of God means the nature of God. God is Love, and therefore God cannot wish for you anything unloving. God is Absolute Peace, and He cannot wish for you discord, chaos, and confusion. God is Life, and Life cannot wish death; that would be a contradiction of its own nature. God is Absolute Joy and cannot wish grief or sorrow. God is Absolute and Unalloyed Harmony and cannot wish sickness or disease. God is Infinite Riches of All Kinds and cannot wish poverty; to think so would be a form of insanity.

God's will for you is something transcending your fondest dreams. The will of God, as Judge Troward, author of *Edinburgh Lectures* and other works on Mental Science, so eloquently puts it, is the tendency of God, and God being Life cannot wish anything detrimental to Itself. Life feels Itself to be Love, Joy, Peace, Beauty, and Its tendency is to express Its own nature which is the same yesterday, today, and forever. When a man says, "I am poor; I am sick; I am weak; I am tired; I am broke; etc.," he brings these conditions on himself by his negative destructive statements.

The name of God is given as I AM in the third chapter of Exodus. I AM is a nameless name. It means Existence, Being, Life, Awareness, Unconditioned Consciousness. It is the Only Presence, the Only Power, and the Cause of All. God creates all things by first imagining Himself to be these things, and then He feels Himself to be that which He imagined Himself to be—this is the way all things are made. Man creates the same way God creates, but he should follow God's pattern of harmony, health, peace, wholeness, beauty, order, symmetry, and right action. Whatever man imagines and feels to be true is brought forth in his life. This is why man should imagine only whatsoever things are lovely and of good report. Whatever man attaches to the I AM within him, he becomes. Therefore man should never say, "I am inferior; I am a failure; etc." To do so is to manifest such states.

The Life Principle as it flows through you takes the shape of the mental mold which you prepare for It. Let us take the analogy of water, which will take the shape of any vessel into which it is poured, yet it ever remains the same H_2O, regardless of the shape and size of the container. Your thoughts, imagery, and mental patterns mold, fashion, and shape your life.

You are here to grow, expand, and unfold, and if all your faculties were fully developed when you were born, you would never discover yourself. If, for example, you were compelled to love your husband or wife, you would have no free will. This is why you say, "I choose _____ from all the women in the world to be my lawful wedded wife." You are not an automaton, you have freedom to give love or retain it. You have the capacity to choose, select, and arrive at a decision through your capacity to reason. In the beginning, man looks out at the three-dimensional world and is governed by appearances and conditions until he awakens to the fact that, through the medium of his own thought and feeling, he can control and direct his life. Gradually man awakens to the Truth that circumstances and conditions are effects and not causes. All outer conditions are subject to change. As man changes his mind he changes his body, environment, and conditions.

Thy will be done on earth as it is in Heaven.

A wonderful prayer! Realize that God's will is always being expressed through you at all times. Make a habit of affirming that God's will is being expressed in all departments of your life, making certain, of course, that you know what you mean when you say, "God's will be done."

God is Boundless Love, Absolute Bliss, Indescribable Beauty, Infinite Intelligence, Absolute Harmony, Omnipotent, Supreme, and Absolute Peace. There are no divisions or quarrels in the absolute. God is Infinitely Good, Perfect, and the Author only of Perfect Good. Pray aright in this way, "God's will is being made manifest in my life as harmony, perfect health, happiness, peace, joy, abundance, love, and perfect divine expression. It is wonderful!"

If you meditate on the above prayer regularly, your present environment and circumstances will magically change and be transformed into the likeness of what you are contemplating. Now, when you say, "God's will is operating in my life," it has a magnificent and beautiful significance full of spiritual precious stones. When you say, "God's plan is made manifest in my life," that too, has a new and wonderful meaning. God's plan is God's will, and His plan can only be beauty, order, symmetry, love, health, and all the good things of life. God's plan for you could only be to express more of Himself through you moving ever onward, upward, and Godward. *Jesus said, As thou has believed, so be it done unto thee.*

It is a magnificent prayer and superb spiritual strategy to say, "God's will be done," particularly when you understand the spiritual significance of these words. If you enthrone in your mind the definite idea that God's will is operating in all your affairs, this constructive belief in your mind will govern your life and cause you to act and express yourself as you believe. Your dominant conviction dictates, governs, and controls your entire life. It is a wonderful thing to know, as Quimby expressed it, that "man is belief expressed." When you know that the Light and Love of God are guiding and governing you in all your ways, you are automatically protected from making errors in judgment, unwise decisions, and wasting your time and efforts along useless lines of endeavor.

A British pilgrim to Lourdes, who was staying with his boy in the hotel where I was said, "If it is God's will, my boy will be healed." I said to him, "God's will for the boy must, by the nature of God, be perfect health for the boy." *I am come that they might have life, and that they might have it more abundantly.* JOHN 10:10. *Therefore I say unto you, what things soever you desire, when ye pray, believe that ye receive them, and ye shall have them.* MARK 11:24. And notice, *whatsoever* is the word. It does not designate anything limited. This marvelous promise of the Bible says, *Whatsoever things you desire, believe you have received them, and you shall have them.*

This man seemed to think that God's will for his boy must be something unpleasant or evil. What a monstrous concept of God! When you say, "If," it means you are full of doubt, fear, and anxiety. There is no "if" in prayer. Cross it out! Never, never say, "If it is God's will," or "If it is right for me." What isn't right for you? Do you have two Gods or one? When you pray for right action, there is only right action. If you are thinking wrong action, you have two powers, God and a devil. Begin to place the true God back on the throne of His glory in your mind.

This father realized immediately what prayer really meant and he said, "I now know what God's will for my boy is, and I am going to claim it, feel it, and believe it until it becomes a part of my consciousness. When I reach a conviction in my mind, my will or desire becomes God's will or the conviction that 'It is done.'"

A remarkable change took place in the boy as the father began to pray meaningfully and with deep understanding, "God's Healing Power is made manifest in the mind and body of my son, and God walks and talks in him."

I have heard this expression frequently, "I want it if God wants me to have it." If you really believe that God is the Divine Presence or Life within you and is Infinite Intelligence and All-Powerful, and is Boundless Love, why should you think that God did not want you to have it, whether it is health, peace, joy, true place, abundance, new home, marriage, or what not?

Many people utter another superstitious phrase, "Maybe it isn't good for me." When people use such an expression, they are living in a world of duality, of two powers. They have God and a devil, they are double-minded. Isn't happiness good for you? Surely, you must agree that God wants you to be happy. If you pray for right action, why would you begin to think of wrong action? There is only a Principle of Right Action in the world. There is no principle of wrong action. There is a Principle of Joy, none of sadness. There is a Principle of Love, none of hatred. There is a Principle of Truth, and none of error. There is a Principle of Harmony, and none of discord.

What kind of a God would you have that did not want you to be joyous, free, radiant, and illumined? You are here to reproduce all the qualities, attributes, potencies, and aspects of God and to move from glory to glory.

And he said unto him, Son, thou are ever with me, and all that I have is thine. LUKE 15:31.

If you have a desire for healing, for true expression, for greater wisdom and spiritual understanding, or for greater wealth and expression to do the things you want to do, surely there is not a doubt in your mind but that God wants you to have all these things. If you think that God wants you to be sick or is testing you in some strange way, or if you think that God could create sickness, such a God is not worthy of your consideration and attention, and the belief is only a false, superstitious concept in your mind.

God wants you to be prosperous as well as healthy. Many people, because of false theological beliefs implanted in their subconscious minds when they were young and impressionable, believe that there is some virtue in lack and limitation. You must eradicate that false belief from your subconscious mind and realize that the Infinite Riches of God are all around you. You cannot count the sands on the seashore or the stars in the heavens above. Did you ever try to count the flowers by the wayside as you drive along the road? Everywhere you look you see a profusion of God's wealth. God's ideas are infinite, and you can have an idea now that could put a million men to work. Ideas are wealth. An invention is an idea in the mind, so is a book, a new business venture, a new real estate project. Men today are proving that they can look at a vast desert and make it rejoice and blossom as the rose. Nature is lavish, extravagant, and bountiful. Man in his greed and lust creates an artificial shortage, but there is no shortage of God's wisdom or creative ideas in the mind of man, if he will become open and receptive to the Divine Influx, which is always ready and available.

Believe that your supply is from God and that He supplies all your needs at every moment of time and point of space. The external world, economic conditions, stock market fluctuation, inflation or deflation, or opinions of man cannot touch you when you are lifted up in consciousness—that dimension of spiritual awareness, where you believe in your heart that your supply is truly and literally from God and nowhere else. The channels through which you receive your wealth are not the source, and you should not confuse the two. You should be completely free in your economic living and prospered in all your ways.

You are not glorifying God when sick, frustrated, neurotic, unhappy, and poverty stricken. You are here to dramatize, portray, and express in your life that which is true of God. To believe in a God of Love is to express love, and to believe in a God of Abundance is to express the abundant life. *According to your belief is it done unto you.* If you have a desire to write a play, write a novel, build a new house, would it not be extremely foolish for you to think that God did not want you to write the play or novel, or build the house? God is within you and your desire to express is from God. God gave you your brain, your mind, the hands to write, also the urge to achieve and express, plus the intelligence and capacity to do all these things.

Imagine saying, "If God wants me to write a play, He will let me know." This would be the quintessence of absurdity. *It is the Father within, He doeth the works.* Your idea or desire must be appropriated in consciousness and felt as true, and when it is accepted subconsciously, then the subconscious will bring it to pass. Your conscious wish or desire has now passed from mere wishing and desiring to a subconscious conviction. The law of the subconscious is one of compulsion, and the will of the subconscious comes to pass. *Not my will* (idea, desire, plan), *but Thy will be done* (my conviction or consciousness) which automatically comes to pass. Our subconscious convictions and beliefs dictate and control all our conscious actions. The subconscious is the power that moves the world.

The dictionary defines will as choice, intention, inclination, determination, tendency, and in order to make it the will of Omnipotence you must animate it, make it alive within you by enthusiasm, feeling, and animation until it becomes embodied in the subconscious mind. When man learns to choose wisely, he will choose happiness, peace, security, joy, health, abundance, and all the blessings of life. He will enthrone the spiritual values and truths of God in his mind and busy his mind with these eternal verities until they become a part of his consciousness in the same manner as an apple becomes a part of his blood stream.

Choose Divine Guidance, Right Action, Divine Order, and Divine Success in your life. What is true of God is true of you for God indwells you. God is always successful, whether making a star, planet, tree, or cosmos. Therefore you were born to succeed as the Infinite cannot fail. The worldly minded man who is a victim of the race mind unconsciously chooses sickness, misfortune, lack, and limitation of all kinds. He fails to realize that thoughts are things, that what he imagines, he becomes, and what he feels he attracts. If man does not do his own thinking, the newspapers, the neighbors, and the race mind will do his thinking for him, and his life will be a mess.

Choose ye this day, whom ye will serve. JOSHUA 14:15.

Choose Life, Love, Truth, and Beauty. Choose Wisdom, and you will find that all Its ways are pleasantness, and all Its paths are peace. You can misuse and misapply any law. You can misuse electricity, chemistry, or any force in nature. The good and evil you experience are the movements and actions of your own mind relative to the Life-Principle, which is forever pure and perfect in Itself.

A man came to see me some time ago. He was an alcoholic and said that if he took one drink he should be compelled to keep on drinking until he fell unconscious on the floor. In other words, he had lost control and was compelled by the law of his subconscious mind to drink. His story was a familiar one. His wife divorced him because of his infidelity. He resented her action and hated her because she refused to take him back. Then he turned to drink to relieve the psychic pain in the same way you might take aspirin for a headache. He repeated this act over and over again, and each time he took a drink to bolster up his spirits, he was rejecting the Power of God within him and suggesting weakness and inferiority to his subconscious mind.

Habits are formed by repeating certain thought patterns or actions over and over again until they establish patterns in the subconscious mind, where they grow until they reach the point of saturation. He now has a psychic bartender established in his subconscious mind that reminds him repeatedly, "You need a drink." When he takes one, he is off to the races; in other words, he has lost control. His wish or conscious will is not to drink, but the will of the subconscious now takes over and says, "You must drink." He has lost control. His choice to drink, which he repeated over and over again until it became an established habit pattern, is now in control.

He can reverse the pattern and be free by the use of the same law which made him a compulsive drinker. Regularly and systematically he contemplates freedom and peace of mind, claiming that his food and drink are God's ideas, which constantly unfold within him, bringing him harmony, health, and peace. He runs a movie in his mind several times daily by imagining himself free, happy, and joyous. He pictures himself doing what he longs to do and hears a friend congratulate him on his freedom and sobriety. Whenever he is tempted, he flashes the movie in his mind and knows that the Power of the Almighty is flowing through his mental movie, and that by a process of mental and spiritual osmosis the mental image is sinking down into his subconscious, where it is being developed in the dark room of his mind. Impressions are made in the subconscious by repetition, faith, and expectancy, and as he continues faithfully imagining his freedom and peace of mind, the day breaks and the shadows flee away. His will (desire for complete freedom from the destructive habit) has become God's will (his deep abiding conviction lodged in the subconscious mind), and he is compelled to express freedom, for the Law of the subconscious is compulsion. The law which held him in bondage is the same law which freed him, enabling him to enter into the glorious liberty of the sons of God.

Thy will be done on earth as it is in Heaven is a wonderful prayer as you now realize. *Heaven* means your own mind or mental and spiritual awareness. What you feel as true in the heavens of your own mind, you shall experience on earth or the objective plane (body, world, environment, circumstances).

Your *will* is your capacity to define your objectives, to choose your goal, ideal, or plan. Live with it mentally by loving it, nursing it, giving it your attention and whole-souled devotion. Finally, it becomes jelled within you and *your will has become God's will,* or the joy of the answered prayer. It is wonderful!

3

The Love That Casts Out Fear

We are told in the Book of Proverbs that The fear of the Lord is the beginning of wisdom.

When you learn the laws of electricity, you are very careful how you apply them because you know the consequences. You know if you put your hand on a naked wire or cause a short circuit what will happen. You learn the theories about insulation and conductivity resulting in a healthy respect and reverence for these laws, and you will follow the nature of the principles.

Likewise, when you learn the principles of chemistry, you have a very healthy respect for the combination of chemicals, their atomic weight, etc., because you also know the disastrous consequences of mixing things together when you do not know the results. For instance, if you mix nitric acid and glycerine together, you will have a powerful explosive.

Fear is a reverence, a healthy respect. You have a healthy respect for the law when you learn the consequences of misusing it. You have a healthy respect for fire, so you do not put your finger into it. Similarly, when men know that their mind is a principle, like the principle of chemistry and physics, they have a very healthy respect for the subconscious mind. They learn that they can use it two ways.

A principle is the way a thing works. We realize that God also is principle. Principle does not change. God is Boundless Love, Infinite Intelligence, and has all the elements of personality. Nevertheless, God works by Law; therefore, we have to work by Law. This Law never changes.

Water runs down hill. It expands when frozen, taking the shape of any vessel into which it is poured. These, and many other characteristics, determine the principle by which water operates. Therefore, we learn that it runs down hill. Your mind operates in the same way. If you think good, good follows. If you think evil, evil follows. If you say, "God can heal me now, God can help me out of this situation," your words betray you. You should say and know, "God is helping and solving my problem now." You would never make the former statement if you knew the way God works.

Man sometimes uses his mind to oppose his good. He has a vivid imagination of things that he does not want. Oftentimes man is looking at obstacles, delays, and difficulties in his mind and he is vividly picturing these things. Then he turns around and says, "God can help me out of this problem." It does not work that way.

Pray this way, "God is helping me now, for God is the solution." Creative Intelligence is the Way, the Truth, and the Life.

If you say to me, "God can heal me," what are you saying? You are saying, "I am now identified with sickness, pains, and aches," and the pain goes on for years. Instead say, "God is healing me now, this very moment. The Creative Intelligence which made me is healing me now."

You must have a healthy respect for the Law and realize that if you say, "I can't do this," you have faith in failure. Faith is an attitude of mind. Faith is the use you make of your mind. Many people have faith in a devil, that he is going to tempt them and bring harm to them. Others have faith in a hell and in a lake of fire that is waiting for them. This is an attitude of mind, an expectancy, a belief of the mind. How can a man believe in a good future if he fears death, torture, and torment? He cannot. If a man thinks that God is cruel, that God is punishing him, and God has created a hell waiting for him because he has sinned or erred (when he could not help himself anyway, since he has to err for that is the way he grows), that man cannot love God, or the Good. It is impossible because he is fearing the future and after-life. He has a God of fear, but God is a God of Love. Such a man cannot banish fear out of his mind, since he must come back to the unity of the One Power.

Basil King, who wrote *Conquest of Fear,* tells that he was going blind. He took a trip to France. He was a young man, depressed, dejected, feared the future, blindness, old age, and all the rest of it. He said he recalled something that a teacher said years previously: "The Life Principle is indestructible, invulnerable, and eternal. It always brings about the expedient which is an answer to the particular need of any man." He used to think that nature was cruel and raw, and that evil abounded in the world. He had strange concepts of God.

This man said a woman asked him, "What do you think God is?"

He replied in his naivete, simplicity, and immaturity, "There are three supernal beings in the sky and three thrones." She laughed at him.

"I knew," he said, "that moment, I had a wrong concept." Then he began to think the Life Principle within him had overcome every obstacle in the world, whether it was a flood, volcanic eruption, war and destruction of all kinds. The Life Principle goes on invulnerable, eternal. Nothing can destroy it. The Life Principle gives fur to the animals in the North. In the South, in the Temperate Zone, it gives them hair, covers others with shells to preserve them. Others are given a poisonous fluid which they emit when attacked. It takes care of all forms of life, such as those that came out of the sea. It gave them legs, made them stand upright, etc., and gave some wings to fly in the air. Always, the Life Principle met the particular need. When primitive man met the tiger, he was frozen with fear. Gradually there came to his aid the dawn of reason, imagination, and memory. (There was a time when man had no memory). Later, man began to think, and this Power within him responded to his thought.

Basil King, in meditating and musing on the Power within, discovered that the Natural Principle, or Life, or Nature is not cruel, but when he combined or united with this Principle in thought, mighty forces came to his aid. He no longer believed in three supernal beings sitting on a throne, but he perceived that God was the Life Principle in him. The average man has pigeon-holed God and brings him out on Sundays, holidays, in cases of death, birth, and marriage, but the rest of the time He is put away in a corner. Some men are afraid to use the term "God." Others look askance when God is mentioned as they begin to think of God in terms of religious connotations because each has a different concept of God, like the blind men of old describing an elephant.

Basil King discarded all the sentimental, preternatural connotations associated with the name of God, and began to realize that God was the Life Principle within him, operating through him, and when he united with this Presence, mighty forces came to his aid. He found God the answer to every problem. He said, "This realization was the beginning of the process of casting out fear which was blinding me and paralyzing me." No man can conquer fear until he comes back to the fact that there is only One Power.

If you want to conquer fear, you have to come back to the Truth that there is One Power, indivisible, and Its source is Love. It has no opposition. It is the Life Principle that has overcome every opposition in this world and goes on conquering and to conquer. There is nothing to oppose It, for It is omnipotent.

Realize you are one with this God Power. You are aligned with It now, and mighty forces will come to your aid. You are one with God, with life, and with all things. *Thou shalt compass me about with songs of deliverance. I will fear no evil for Thou art with me. Thy rod and Thy staff, they comfort me.*

When we are fearful or indulge in negative thoughts, we are vibrating at a very low level. When you meditate on a psalm and say, *The Lord is my shepherd, I shall not want,* or "The Presence of God is right here where I am," or "I will fear no evil for God is with me," or "I dwell in the Secret Place of the Most High," and "God is guiding me now, the Presence of God is with me," you are thinking spiritually.

These spiritual thoughts are of a very high frequency and are of a very high vibration. What happens to the evil negative thoughts of fear, destruction, and disaster? These are destroyed and neutralized. You are now vibrating at a higher level. You are vibrating at a spiritual frequency, and just like you put your finger on a tuning fork, that is the end of the negative vibration. That is the end of the evil because evil is a false belief about God and His Infinite Goodness.

When we are full of fear, we have greater faith in evil than in God; this is shocking, but it is true. Fear is God upside down. Fear is faith in the wrong thing. You have faith that the sun will rise in the morning. You have faith that you can drive your car. You have faith that you will get an answer to your prayer when you pray for guidance, but many people have faith in the wrong thing. There are people who are looking forward to misfortune. There are people working in offices who are afraid of their jobs, afraid they are going to lose their money, and of what is going to happen to them when they grow old, instead of realizing,

"I am always in my true place, for God is my employer. I am working for Him and I live forever."

A pilot said to me, "I am never afraid when I navigate a plane, whether I go north, south, east, or west, for I am a pilot for God. I am flying for Him, and I am as safe in the sky as on the earth. Nothing can happen to me. It is impossible."

That man has faith in the Goodness of God, in the right action of God, in the guidance of God. He has faith in the Eternal Principle, and in the immutable, changeless Laws of God. Faith is your attitude of mind, what you expect, what you are focusing on, the things that you are vividly imagining.

Some people are afraid of old age, some are afraid of death, but that which they are afraid of does not exist. You are alive; you are alive with the Life of God. You are alive now. God is Life Eternal. Because God lives, you live. God cannot die; therefore, you cannot die.

Realize God is your employer. He is always taking care of you, loves you, and you are always in your true place. When someone makes negative statements about you, begin to dwell on the above Truths, and you will always be taken care of. "I will fear no evil for Thou art with me. Thy rod and Thy staff, they comfort me." "Perfect Love casteth out fear, for fear has a torment. He that feareth is not made perfect in love."

Dr. Brunt of Capetown, South Africa, told me about a frail woman about eighty years of age. A little granddaughter came to live with her. Her parents were killed out in the jungle somewhere. She said this woman loved this little child, and would go through fire and water for her because that is what you do when you are in love. There was a poisonous snake about to hypnotize the child (for that is what a snake does, it hypnotizes you), and this frail woman seized some branches of a tree and killed the snake. Her fear of the snake was swallowed up in victory and triumph. Love casts out fear. She had that all-embracing mood of love to save that child at all costs which cast out her fear.

Love is always outgoing. It is an emanation. Fear is turning within in morbid introspection, believing someone is going to hurt you or that evil spirits can possess you. When any person believes in external powers, he denies the one God. God is within you, and moves as a Unity. It is the Life Principle within you forever seeking to express Itself as Love, Peace, Bliss, Joy and Right Action.

When we are fearful, we are very selfish in the wrong way. Fear is a morbid introspection. Cease building a wall around yourself saying, "I am going to get hurt. These people are against me. God is against me." Many people are over-concerned with themselves. To say, "I won't go anywhere, I might get hurt" is morbid selfishness.

Love is always outgoing. Love must have an object. You can fall in love with music, art, a great project, etc. You can fall deeply in love with the Truths of the Bible. You can become absorbed and engrossed in science and many other things.

Einstein loved the principle of mathematics. He said, "It reveals to me all its secrets." That is what love does. You can fall in love with astronomy, and it will reveal to you all its secrets.

You can readily see, therefore, what love is. It is an outgoing. It must have an object. How much do you want what you want? Do you want to leave your old self with your false concepts and old ideas? Are you willing to get new ideas, new imagery, new viewpoints? Are you open and receptive? Do you want good digestion? If you do, you must give up resentment. You must give up your grudges and peeves. To be made whole, release your fears and hates. You have to leave Los Angeles to go to Denver. Likewise, you have to leave your jealousies, hates, plus your false concepts of God in order to enter into the joy of health and happiness.

How much do you want what you want to be? How much do you love this new ideal? Emerson said, "Do the thing you are afraid to do, and the death of fear is certain." By example, if you are afraid to talk before an audience, get up and talk. After a while you will overcome that fear. Do it again, again, and again.

If you are afraid to swim, look at the water and say, "I am going to conquer you. God is love, and I am in charge of my own thoughts, my own feelings, and my own responses." You are a king; you are the master. Are the thoughts, ideas and images in your mind going to master you, or are you going to master them? Are you the employer? Yes, you are. You can order your thoughts around and tell them to give attention to your ideal and the Truths of God which were always true.

Focus your attention on that which is good, that which is true, that which heals and blesses you. You can determine your own response to whatever happens, to the headlines in the newspapers, and to what people say. You are the master. You are a king in charge of your mind, responses, thoughts, ideas, and imagery. You are the absolute master. You are the God over your own realm. "I will make you God, to Pharaoh."

You mold and fashion your own destiny. There are no external forces. You are the absolute monarch over your own world, and you are in complete charge. You can enter into the glorious liberty of the sons of God, but you must know how. Where is the fear if you are a god in your own world, which you are?

The thing man fears does not exist. It exists only as a thought in his mind. An actor was saying to himself, "I am going to fail. I am going to strike the wrong note. I am going to say the wrong thing." His vivid imagination was on failure. He had to fall in love with a new concept of himself, and he became the great artist that he now is. He fell in love with the new concept, the new estimate, the new blueprint of himself. Fear means you are wrapped up in your own shortcomings and thinking too much about your inadequacies.

Think of the Greatness within you. All fear is based upon the fact that you are thinking from the standpoint of inferiority, weakness, and inadequacy, instead of thinking from the standpoint of the Infinite God within you which is the Power that moves in the world. When you are presented with an assignment, realize, "I do this through the Power of God which moves through me." Tremendous powers will come in response to that attitude. "Act as though I am, and I will be." Act as though you believe that this Power is here, and that It will come to your aid.

This actor had to fall in love with a new estimate of himself. Love is a fascination. You become entranced, fascinated, and absorbed; moreover, you become emotionally involved because love is an emotional attachment. Therefore, you become attached to the ideals and goals of life. You can fall in love with your goal, and all fear will go away. Fall in love with something now.

Fall in love with a nobler, sweeter, grander concept of yourself. Fall in love with the Greater Self within you. Dwell on Its tremendous potentialities and qualities. Let God's Power captivate your imagination. Let it thrill you through and through, for love causes you to unite with your ideal. You don't try to hold the ideal; it holds you entranced. That is love; then all fear goes away. Fear is swallowed up in love. Love and fear cannot dwell together. The reason people hate and are jealous is that they have a false concept of God. If anyone thinks that there is a lake of fire, and that God is judging him, or is punishing him, or that the stars are governing him, I want to say frankly, categorically, and incisively, such a concept is atheistic. It is the denial of the Presence, the Power, the Omnipotence, and the Love of God.

We know there is no power but God, and there are no divisions or quarrels in It; therefore, let us align ourselves with God. We do not try to change God. God is constant; God is invariable. Man is variable and inconstant. The Truths of God remain the same yesterday, today, and forever. "Who shall hurt you if you are a follower of that which is good?" "No evil shall befall the just." "If God be for you, who can be against you?" "There is no fear in love. Perfect love casteth out fear."

You are told over and over again in Genesis that *The Lord giveth the increase,* and whatever you give attention to, negative or positive, your subconscious mind magnifies and multiplies it beyond your imagination. Therefore, if you dwell on loss, loss comes to you. Perhaps it comes in loss of prestige, health, finances, family, or in business. And if you continue with this negative pattern, of course, what you fear most comes upon you. If your faith is in loss, that is inverted faith, isn't it? Do not have faith in the gloomy, morbid aspect of things instead, have faith in the real Truths of God.

Isn't it far more interesting, fascinating, alluring, and captivating to contemplate the things which are good? Eat the blessed bread of the Blessed God by imagining perfect health and happiness, and by contemplating the Truths of God which are also true of you. Practice the Love that casts out fear.

Fall in love. Love is a principle of life. When fear comes, move to the opposite. Fear is a signal to do something. When you are cold, you build a fire; therefore, do not stay frozen at this end of the pendulum. Affirm, "God is here. God is with me now." Realize His Presence, His rod—the Power, His staff—your authority, to wield this Power. It is right there with you.

A girl taking an examination in school said that her knees were shaking with fear. She decided to overcome the fear and said to herself, "The Lord is my shepherd. God is right here. God is my peace. The Peace of God flows through me. The Love of God is here, and there is right action. I am at peace. The poise and the harmony of God are here." She moved to the opposite. That is the Law of Substitution. Begin to think of the Eternal Verities. Impress them on your mind. You do it with feeling and with understanding; then the fear goes away. You have supplanted it; it is the Law of Substitution.

Probably you read about the soldier in the Korean War. He said bullets were falling all around him, and he was all alone. He was shaking with fright, and all he could remember were a few passages from the Psalms. *Under His wings shall I rest, and The Lord is my light and my salvation. The Lord is the strength of my life, of whom shall I be afraid?* As he dwelt on these Truths he said, "Faith and an inner sense of peace and poise came to me." He found his way to safety and back to his company. Had he remained frozen at that point of fear, he would have been doomed, paralyzed, and unable to flee; but he moved to the opposite.

When fear comes, it is the Divine Self in you telling you there is something wonderful waiting to come into your experience. It means the end of the old condition, and the birth of the new.

All parents should find out what their children are being taught, because they must not permit teachers to brainwash, mesmerize, and hypnotize their children with devils, demons, and falsehoods which bedevil them. They should be taught about a God of Love. They should be instructed to release the Imprisoned Splendor, that they are children of God, that God never deserts His creation, that He cares for them and loves them, that He is the Life Principle within them, and that God loves to manifest Himself through all men. That is why you have Divine impulses and the reason why you want to conquer, explore, sing, and dance, because it is God seeking to express beauty, harmony, rhythm and wisdom through you.

Fear thoughts, worry thoughts, negative thoughts, thoughts of war, etc., will not hurt you unless you entertain them for a long period of time, and except you emotionalize them deeply; otherwise, they will not hurt you in the slightest. They are potential trouble for you, but they are not actualized. Remember that whatever idea you emotionalize becomes impressed in your subconscious, and the subconscious brings it to pass.

Wives sit at home and fear that they are going to lose their husbands. Husbands are afraid they are going to lose their wives. Mothers are afraid they are going to lose their sons, their jobs, and everything else under the sun. All these things do not exist. They are morbid pictures in the mind. There is no law on earth which compels people to think of these negative things. This negative imagining is a distorted, twisted, diabolical perversion of their God-given faculty of imagination.

Why should any mother in the world think evil of her own son? Why should she think because he is late getting home that he has been run over by a truck, that he is in the hospital being operated on, that he has fallen into a pool? Why not surround him with the Presence of God and say, "Where he is, God is, and God's Love surrounds him. Where God is, there is no accident or death; there is only Love, and the whole Armour of God is where he is." Nothing can ever happen to that child because his mother loved him.

Prayer is a realization of the Presence of God where the person is, and that is the Presence of Harmony, Peace, Love, Bliss, and Joy. You do not pray for protection, for if you do, you have a God of fear. I do not pray that a person is protected because if I do, it means that I have another power opposing God. I realize the Divine Presence is where the person is, and realize the Love of God is there.

If a man will sit down frequently and go back to the simple Truths that God is guiding him, that there is right action in his life, and that the Love of God is flowing through him, then the Wisdom of God will reveal to him what to do. The Healing Presence of God will be released in his body, and Infinite Intelligence will give him all the ideas necessary to handle the problems of the day. This is resting in God. He is asking for guidance and direction, and when he communes with the Divine Presence, Mighty Forces come to his aid. Man will no longer be anxious or disturbed when he thinks from the standpoint of the Infinite One, the Power that moves the world. Cease thinking from the superimposed standpoint of fear, ignorance, doubt, anxiety, and false concepts.

The answer to all fear is to realize that God is, that He is right where you are, that there is no power to challenge God, that one with God is a majority, and if God be for you, who can be against you? No one!

Realize that there are no enemies outside, that the universe is friendly, that God is friendly. When you are friendly with God and when you love the Source which created you, and when you are grateful, you can hate no man. Fall in love with the Truths of God, and you will find that the whole universe responds to you. Come back to the simple Truth which an ancient mystic discovered in silent meditation: "Let nothing disturb you. Everything in this world passes away, but God. God alone is sufficient."

4

Removing Mental Stumbling Blocks

The solution lies within the problem. The answer is in every question. If you are presented with a difficult situation, and you cannot see your way clear, the best procedure is to assume that Infinite Intelligence which knows all and sees all has the answer and is revealing it to you now. Your new mental attitude that Creative Intelligence is bringing about a happy solution will enable you to find the answer. When you begin—God begins. Rest assured that such an attitude will bring order, plan, and meaning to all your undertakings.

The Bible says, *Behold I send an Angel before thee, to keep thee in the way, and to bring thee into the place which I have prepared.* EXODUS 23:20. This means that your mood of faith and confidence in an Almighty

Power moving on your behalf goes before you to make straight, joyous, and perfect your way.

I will lift up mine eyes unto the hills, from whence cometh my help. PSALM 121:1. Cease whining, crying, complaining, and moaning; this attitude will only add to your misery, suffering, and lack. Instead, envision your good, the way that you want things to be. Rehearse your knowledge about the Great Truths of Life. Rise up mentally above the hardships and difficulties and think of God and His Wisdom. Then you will generate a tremendous liberating, healing force which will inspire you, open doors, reveal new ways, plans, and supply you with all your needs for the accomplishment of your goals.

You can change your whole life, if you really want to. You must give up resentment and ill will in order to have good digestion and perfect health. You must give up the lesser for the greater if you want to advance and move forward in life.

I knew a young lady who had a beautiful singing voice, but she was constantly demeaning, demoting, and criticizing herself by saying, "I do not have a chance. I am too old. I do not know the right people."

She had to cease condemning herself in order to get what she wanted. She decided to fall in love with a new concept of herself. She imagined that she was singing before an audience and she became entranced, fascinated, and absorbed in the joy of it all. A new door of expression opened for her because she gave up her old way of thinking and affirmed the Truth about herself.

How much do you really want to be a new person? Do you really want to change conditions, experiences, and your whole personality? The first requirement is that you must come to a clear-cut, definite decision in your mind that you are going to transform your life. You must desire to change with all your heart and cease being a propaganda machine idly repeating all the old stereotyped concepts, ideas, and beliefs implanted in your subconscious mind since birth.

A woman wrote me to the effect that she was about to divorce her husband because he was so tyrannical in the home and that her children were terrified of him. In talking to him, I discovered that he was the victim of long repressed fears. Moreover, his father was unduly harsh and strict with him. He resented his father very much even though the latter had long since passed on to the next dimension of life.

He understood my diagnosis which was that I believed he was unconsciously trying to retaliate with his own father by his despotic, tyrannical attitude toward his own children. The man had to desire to change himself in order to save his marriage.

He released his father through prayer by wishing for him peace, and all the blessings of life. He continued in this manner until all the roots of hatred were withered. He adopted a pattern of prayer by meditating at three specific periods—morning, afternoon, and evening. Finally, he discovered that prayer was a good habit. He changed his thoughts and kept them changed. As a result, his home is peaceful and happy, and his children love him. It is possible to unwind that tangled skein and get at the significant core.

A husband started divorce proceedings against his wife. His main complaint was that she was too extravagant. In talking to her, I discovered that she had never received any appreciation, understanding, or approbation from her husband. She felt very insecure and was actually trying to purchase with money the deep inner sense of security which she had always lacked. They decided to become real partners. He shared a complete knowledge of his business assets with her and showed her that she was well provided for in case something should happen to him. They began to pray together every night for harmony, health, peace, God's guidance, right action, and all their difficulties were dissolved in the light of God's Love.

Let God's Love come into your thoughts, words, and actions, and your whole world will magically melt in the image and likeness of your inner contemplation. You will sometimes find that the seeming problems of gargantuan proportions can be reduced to a size so infinitesimal that it seems laughable.

There are alcoholics who do not want a healing; they do not want to give up their mental stumbling blocks, such as grudges, peeves, self-condemnation, resentments, and ill-will. When an alcoholic admits to the fact that he is an alcoholic and has a strong, healthy desire for freedom and peace of mind, he is fifty-one per cent healed. As he envisions his freedom-state, his advancement, and enlargement in the right way, the Power of the Almighty will back him up; then the shakes and the cravings are automatically eliminated for the joy that is set before him.

All of us should begin to remove the old, accepted viewpoints, opinions, and false beliefs implanted in our minds when we were young and impressionable. The average man thinks and expresses the thoughts of dead men; the dead past seems to rule in the minds of millions of people. I talk to men who have not had a new idea or a new viewpoint in fifty years.

Are you a victim of propaganda, or do you think for yourself? A woman told me that she knows exactly how her husband is going to respond to headlines in the paper, to columnists, to certain politicians, and she can even repeat almost word for word his reactions to religious subjects. He is like the children in

Red China who are conditioned to think, speak, act, and react according to a prescribed pattern. These children become like a phonograph which reproduces whatever is on the record. The recording machine is the subconscious mind which faithfully reproduces whatever is impressed upon it.

You are not born to be an automaton. You should think for yourself. Cease letting others think and speak in you and for you. Refuse to let others despoil and pollute your mind with thoughts of fear, sickness, and misfortune. If you have a ready ear and listen to the prejudices and fears of other people, you may contaminate yourself with the same.

The following is an instance where the "dead" spoke and acted through a young father. He was about to divorce his wife because she did not make the children kneel down and pray every night before retiring. His mental block was that he happened to be the son of an overly fastidious city-bred mother who was also somewhat of a religious fanatic. She had insisted on his kneeling down and repeating by rote certain prescribed prayers every night prior to sleep. As a boy he had resented this bedtime procedure and had repressed into his subconscious mind a rebellion against his mother's "punishment."

Psychologically speaking, this young father was trying to get even with his mother by imposing on his two boys the same religious ritual which he as a young boy was compelled to follow. His wife's custom was to teach the two boys a few simple prayers when they were in bed, emphasizing that God was a God of Love and that He would watch over them like a loving father.

I explained to the young father the reason for his resentment toward his wife, pointing out and elucidating on the facts that she had unwittingly frustrated his desire for revenge, thereby incurring his hostile feelings which were projected on her. He realized that the mental block to marital happiness was within himself, consequently he willingly accepted the interpretation.

Some years ago Lord Northcliffe who took over the London Times told about a man who came to the Times Building every Saturday afternoon, entered a certain room which was a bedroom, and remained there until the following Monday morning. Lord Northcliffe questioned the man and asked why he was there. He said that he brought twenty-five pounds of gold for the week-end in case the bank needed it. The amazing fact is that when Lord Northcliffe phoned the bank, they said that other men with the bag of gold had been occupying that room on week-ends for about one hundred years.

The reason for all this was due to an order issued by the owner of the Times during the battle of Waterloo, 1815, which happened to be on a Sunday. At that time the newspaper editor wanted to send men to cover the story and he could not raise sufficient money to cover the expedition. The following day he made an arrangement with a London Bank to send one thousand pounds in gold regularly to the Times Building when the bank closed on Saturday noon. This is an example of a thought of a dead man governing a big banking institution for one hundred years resulting in waste of time, money, and effort.

Are you repeating the same old patterns of thoughts, going through the same mental movements and reactions as you did thirty or forty years ago? Have you asked yourself about your prejudices, fears, biases, and jealousies? Why are they in your mind? Why have you not consulted someone about your abnormal fears? If you did, you would discover that they were a conglomeration of sinister shadows in your mind, and there is no power in a shadow.

Do you say that you have a personal saviour and that you are saved by the blood of the lamb? Where did this weird concept come from? You should check into your religious beliefs and find out their source and origin. Make a definite decision now and that is: Believe nothing that you do not understand. Learn about your subconscious mind and the power of your own thought, and you will discover that the Saving Principle is within yourself.

You do not ride a mule to go to San Francisco like some of your grandfathers did; neither do you send a message to Chicago by pony express. In the same way, you should not permit the dead, superstitious, ignorant beliefs of antecedents to govern, rule, and manipulate your mind. There are many people who think that by the repetition of an incantation their circumstances can be changed without changing their mentality; consequently they are doomed to disappointment.

A business man complained to me that he could not keep employees; therefore he had a constant turnover. I discovered that he had an atrociously bad temper which had driven all his clerks away. He realized that the stumbling block was within himself and he decided to change his thoughts and keep them changed.

He prayed that Infinite Intelligence would attract to him employees who would appreciate and love the work, and also feel that they were adequately compensated. He adopted a pattern of prayer whereby he prayed for the peace, prosperity, and happiness of each employee. He began to radiate love and goodwill to all his customers, his wife, and his children. He made a habit of this, for prayer is a habit. This man has no more trouble with his employees and close business associates.

A man wrote me saying that he had been praying for prosperity in his business for two years, but he had not achieved any results. He had had some glimmerings of spiritual truth, but his attitude of mind of deep-seated resentment toward a business associate who was very prosperous financially automatically and necessarily expressed itself in financial difficulties, sickness, and frustration.

I asked him how much he really wanted what he wanted. Did he desire it enough to give up his hostile attitude? There is no transaction without an exchange. He began to see that he could not attract wealth by condemning what he was praying for and resenting the affluence of his competitor. Frankly I inquired, "Do you prefer resentment and jealousy to prosperity and peace of mind?" Seeing the light, he began to pray for greater success and prosperity for his competitor. Prayer always prospers.

The stumbling block to our health, happiness, and achievement is always in our own mind, and spiritual understanding will cause our circumstances to improve in every respect. Per contra, a want of true spiritual understanding expresses itself in all sorts of difficulties in our life.

If there seems to be an undue delay in getting an answer to your prayer, it may be that the difficulty is deep-seated in your subconscious mind, requiring more prayer work; or you are not praying in the right way. In this case, ask Infinite Intelligence to reveal to you what you need to know.

When a man says that he must have a demonstration by Monday or Tuesday of next week, otherwise the judge will rule against him, or that he will lose his business unless there is an immediate answer, he must remember that God never fails, God is never late, and God is independent of time and space.

Time does not really matter, for prayer gets results irrespective of what the court said on a certain day. You trust God to put everything right regardless of what happened last Monday or Tuesday. You continue knowing that prayer always wins out irrespective and regardless of what may have happened.

"Great peace have they who love thy law and nothing shall offend them." As you love the law that your thought is creative and that the Spirit flows through the patterns of your thought is creative imagery, you will move away from all morbid introspection and negative concepts. When the impulse to despondency comes, it will stimulate you to think of true goals and ideals whereby you give your energy to your desires, aspirations, and ambitions rather than to conditions and circumstances.

Love your ideal until you are absorbed and engrossed in it. Let the old and worthless thoughts die. Love the new, the appealing, and elevating patterns of life. The outside world may argue with the inside world of your dreams and ideals. Remember the outside is effect, not cause. Be sure to see to it that the energy, vitality, and power of your belief run with the ideal you seek. Then you are on the way to spiritual maturity. In every adversity is the seed of opportunity.

Emerson said, "Whilst man sits on the cushion of advantages, he goes to sleep. When he is pushed, tormented, defeated, and harassed, he has a chance to learn something. He has been put on his wits, on his manhood. He has gained facts, learned of his ignorance, and is cured of his insanity of conceit."

Stand up to your problems, decide now with equanimity and faith in God to solve them. The door will open, and the way will be shown you.

I would like to mention an experience many seem to have. They start some desirable project, or they set out to accomplish an assignment for an employer, and they find that they are unable to complete it. They say something happens at the last minute, that the man who was to sign dropped dead, or he changed his mind at the eleventh hour. An actress said to me recently that everything went smoothly until she was called to sign the contract, and the producer had a heart attack one half hour previously, so the contract was postponed. Others complain that the sale falls through the moment they are about to sign.

The delay and block is in our own mind. What we fear, we attract. What we expect, we experience. Break the so-called jinx this way: Affirm boldly, "I and my Father are one. God thinks, speaks, and acts through me. There is only One Power, and that Power moves as a unit. No person, place, or thing can interfere with God's work, and my work is God's work, for God works through me. In Him I live, move, and have my being. In me God lives, moves, and expresses Himself fully. God's work cannot be delayed. God is always successful and completes all His undertakings. What is true of God is true of me. I bring all my undertakings to divine fulfillment and fruition in Divine Order through Divine Love."

You must want what you want with sufficient zeal and enthusiasm to take the trouble to learn how to think clearly, lucidly, and spiritually, since thought is the only cause.

Tune in with God, and you will rise triumphantly over all problems for, "He never faileth." "I bore you on eagles' wings, and brought you unto myself."

5

To Be, To Do, And To Have

Whatsoever ye shall ask in my name, that I will do.

To be, to do, and to have—these are God's gifts to you. God is seeking to express Himself through you as your desire. Desire is the gift of God. As Browning said, "'Tis thou, God, who giveth, 'tis I who receive." Desire pushes man. It is the goad of action. It is behind all progress. Desire for health, happiness, true place, abundance, and security—all these are messengers of God, saying to each one of us, "Come on up higher!"

Desire is behind all progress. It is the push of the Life-Principle. Desire causes us to jump out of the way of an oncoming bus. We do this because we have a basic desire to preserve our life. The farmer plants seed due to his desire to attain food for himself and his family. Man builds airplanes and space ships, due to his desire to collapse time and space and explore the world. Desire is an angel of God telling us of something which, if accepted by us, will make our life fuller and happier. The greater the expected benefit from the desire, the stronger is our desire. Where there is no expected benefit, gain, or advancement accruing, there is no desire; consequently, no action is found.

Failure to realize our desires to be, to do, and to have over a long period of time result in frustration and unhappiness. You are here to choose happiness, peace, prosperity, and all the blessings of Heaven. Your desire enables you to say, "This is good, therefore I choose it; however this is negative, so I reject it." All choice implies the perception of something preferable over what is rejected.

The idea which some schools of thought have of annihilating and suppressing desire is disastrous in its consequences. If man succeeded in this, good and evil would be alike to him, for nothing has any power to raise any desire in him. He would become dead to all feeling and to all motive of action. Your desire means you choose one thing in preference to another. Where desire is extinguished, no such capacity to choose can exist.

Troward, author of many mental and spiritual textbooks, points out that Indian devotees, who, in pursuance of their resolve to crush out all desire, both for good and evil alike, become attenuated human forms, hopeless wrecks of what were once living men. Troward points out that extinction of desire means apathy, no feeling, and no action. Desire is the cause of all feeling and action, and is the moving principle of the universe. Desire is the creative power and must be channeled and directed wisely. Desire and its fulfillment take place in your own mind.

There are no evil desires in the true sense. You may misdirect or misinterpret the desire which wells up within you. For example, if you are poor, you desire wealth. If you are sick, you desire health. If you are in prison, you want freedom. You may desire love, companionship, or perhaps true place. The man who desires wealth may, in his ignorance, fulfill his urge or desire by killing a banker or robbing a store. This is misdirection of his desire, and he finds himself in jail and charged with murder. Teach a man that there is an Infinite Intelligence within him which can fulfill his desires, and he overcomes his sense of opposition and frustration. Man's desire for food is legitimate and normal, but killing someone in order to get a loaf of bread breeds violence, opposition, guilt, and self-destruction.

There is a Power within man which will lift him up, set him on the high road to happiness, health, peace of mind, and the realization of his fondest dreams without depriving any other person of God's limitless blessings. A man who was broke, out of work, and frightfully frustrated came to one of our Sunday lectures some time ago and listened to the four steps of prayer. He went home and applied it. He had never heard a lecture on the mind, but he said, "This makes sense." He made a list of three things he wanted; you might call them material, but they were his needs. The items on the list were true place, an automobile, and all the money he needed.

He chose these concrete things to see if his thoughts were things. He wanted to prove to himself that the idea of the thing was the thing itself. I said in the lecture that the idea was the reality back of the form. He established a definite method of working and practiced it conscientiously every day, sticking to it long enough to give it a fair chance. This man knew that you do not learn to swim after one or two attempts.

He prayed for true place as follows: "I know Infinite Intelligence responds to me. It is now revealing my true place to me. I am aware of my hidden talents. I am receiving a wonderful income. I know the idea of true place and its manifestation are one in Divine Mind. I follow the lead which comes."

Within two weeks from the day his experiment began he signed a contract for a job in San Francisco. He gave thanks and rejoiced in the Law of God. Then he went on to the next objective—a new car. He said to me, "I know I have the idea of a car. It is real, and I am going to remain faithful to it. It must manifest." He won a car in a raffle contest. Now he knew the secret of the subconscious that if he identified himself mentally and emotionally with the idea, the subconscious would bring it to pass. He was very thankful. The next request was more wealth. Each morning and evening during his prayer period he gave thanks for God's wealth circulating in his life claiming that his idea of wealth was fulfilled. He fell in love with a wealthy widow in San Francisco, and she financed his new business.

This man established a definite method of working, claiming each of his desires as already fulfilled. He claimed each one separately, but all at the same time during his morning and evening meditative period. If you pray like the above mentioned man, and if no improvement at all shows itself within a couple of weeks, scrap that method and adopt a new one. Remember, there is an answer. That is as certain as the rising of the sun.

Cultivate simplicity and spontaneity, knowing that whatsoever ye shall ask in prayer, believing, ye shall receive. Decide now that you can do what you long to do and that you can be what you wish to be. No enlightened person today believes that a cruel fate condemns us to sickness, misery, or suffering. There is nothing holding us in mediocrity, in ill health, or in a miserable condition, but our own thoughts and false belief.

Come out of the prison of fear, want, and loneliness. Cease thinking that God visits illness upon you for some strange reason, or that you must endure the sickness or be resigned to it. It is blasphemy to say that God is punishing you. It is also blasphemy to blame God for your sickness. Your mind and body are one. In the field of psychosomatic medicine they realize it is impossible to tell where the mind begins and the body ends. Research work today reveals that the hidden, underlying causes of physical maladies lie in the tangled depths of the mind, in frustrated rages, in baffled desires, in jealousies, and anxieties. Don't blame God for troubles we bring on ourselves by our own wrong thinking or our failure to think at all.

A girl said to me that all she desired was Wisdom. That is the over-all desire of everyone, but our terminology is not the same. When you have Wisdom, you are expressing yourself fully here and now. An automobile is a spiritual idea in front of your door. A ham sandwich, when you are hungry, is an answer to your prayer and also is spiritual. If you sing well on the stage, it is just as spiritual as a man singing the 23rd Psalm in the choir. The man who repairs the roof of your house is performing spiritual labor just as well as a minister, priest, or rabbi who may be reading a text from the Bible or broadcasting a sermon.

Realize that the spirit and body are one. Cease looking down your nose at material things. Stop once and for all, separating the Spirit of God from the flesh and blood of the world. Every physical act, no matter how base you may consider it, is the Living Spirit within you animating material form. You are not degraded or bemeaned when you scrub a dirty floor or clean stables. If you are condemning anything in this world, you are demoting and depreciating yourself.

Good and bad are in your own thought, and you color everything in the universe by the way you think and feel. Do not criticize, condemn, or despise your body or the world. Your body is the temple of the Living God, and the whole wide world is the body of God. The world is the Dance of God and the Song of God.

A man in Los Angeles had an ulcerated leg for five or six years. It would heal up for a time and then break out again. He said his father had the same thing, and that he supposed it was hereditary, and that he had resigned himself to it. He learned that was the wrong thing to do. He became aware of the fact that the Creative Intelligence which made his body never loses interest in that which It creates. He learned that the

Healing Presence is within him and that the process of digestion, assimilation, and circulation are carried on by this Healing Presence. This man stopped fearing and expecting a relapse. For about five or ten minutes in the morning and evening he affirmed with deep understanding, "I have a Silent Partner, a Healing Presence who knows how to heal, and His Healing Presence is bringing about the beauty of wholeness now. I believe now that my Silent Partner is saturating my whole being with Its love, beauty, and perfection."

This slight alteration in his approach led him out of the lameness and pain into radiant health. God wants your best performance. Adopt a pragmatic standpoint and affirm boldly, "The Infinite Intelligence which created me knows the process of healing. It is healing me now in Divine Order. I believe, I accept, and I rejoice because my Silent Partner is responding now."

This attitude is sound, and it will work. We follow the desire which captivates and holds our attention. All of us find ourselves moving in the direction of the idea which dominates our mind for the time being. A burning desire to be and to do will start you off on the high-road to success and achievement. John Bunyan had an intense desire to reveal the truth about religion, and his deeper mind responded. Though he was in prison at the time and sorely punished, he brought forth the masterpiece, "Pilgrim's Progress."

The oak sleeps in the acorn. The bird waits in the egg, and God is waiting in you to be expressed and reproduced on the screen of space. Edison was a "tramp" telegraph operator, and though he was deaf and expelled from school, he had an intense desire to light up the world. The Living Intelligence within him responded to his faith and belief.

Dress up your desire, exalt it in your own mind, beautify it, magnify it, let it captivate you so much that you yearn for it. Fall in love with your desire. The mental picture you have in your mind backed up by faith will be manifested by the subconscious mind.

A woman in our audience had tried unsuccessfully to sell a home in another state for over three years. One Sunday morning in this service she got into a drowsy, sleepy state, a state akin to sleep. In this relaxed, quiet, peaceful state of mind, she focused all her attention on the sale of the home. She was in a state of physical immobility which increased the power of concentration. In this state she imagined she had the check for the full price in her hand, she gave thanks for the check, and rejoiced in its possession. She was looking backward at the goal, at the fulfilled desire. She rejoiced, gave thanks, and was filled with the feeling, "It is done!" In this mental attitude all effort was reduced to a minimum. That same day in Ohio the broker sold her home. It was about the same time as she was giving thanks for the sale. She said to me, "I knew I let it go this morning because I had a great sense of relief."

There is an old saying in the Tarot Teaching which says, "Man is what he imagines himself to be." Your idea is an image which comes forth spontaneously from your subliminal depths or from the world without. Your faculty of imagination clothes all ideas and projects them on the screen of space. This is why thoughts are things. One is the inside and the other is the outside of the same reality. Quimby said, "Man moves as he is moved upon. Man acts as he is acted upon."

Your ideas govern you and master you. Your idea this morning is tending to execute itself. The primal faculty of man is his imagination. Use it wisely, judiciously, and constructively. Imagine what is lovely and of good report. *Let us make man in our image.* GENESIS 1:26. God imagines Himself to be the sun, moon, stars, world, and man. He then feels Himself to be what He imagined Himself to be. The idea and the feeling unite (male and female), and the cosmos comes forth. God imagined Himself to be man. Then through feeling He became what He imagined Himself to be.

Give life and confidence to your image, and it will become alive in your experience. This is how you become what you want to become. Troward said,

"Whatever you affix to I AM you become." I AM is the Name of God which means pure Being, Awareness, or Life. If you say, "I am sick," you will become sick. If you say, "I am poor," you will become poor. Why unite yourself with the feeling of poverty? Begin to affirm, "I am strong, whole, perfect, powerful, radiant, illumined, and inspired." Feel the truth of what you affirm, and wonders will happen in your life. Do not permit your feeling to unite with an image of limitation as you will generate the consequences of your unholy alliance.

Let us restate some of the salient points of these important truths. You do not put vitality into the seed, but you must deposit it in the soil. You water the seed regularly, thereby accelerating its growth. Let us look at our mind. The seed is your desire to be, to do, or to have. You must deposit it in the receptive soil of your mind, use no force nor mental coercion, and cease trying to make it come to pass. Your job is to keep out the negative thoughts of doubt and fear which tend to neutralize your affirmative prayer. Enter into the feeling of pleasure and satisfaction in imagining the fulfillment of your desire.

Your desire or idea is the substance of things hoped for, and the evidence of things not seen. Your desire is as real as your hand or heart, and has its own form, shape, and substance in another dimension of mind.

"Believe that ye have it now, and ye shall receive it." Regard your mental creation or idea as a spiritual reality. Then implicitly trust the Law of growth to bring it to pass and walk in the Light that it is so, until the day breaks and the shadows flee away.

6

The Mysteries And Wonders Of Sleep

For God speaketh once, yea twice, yet man per-
ceiveth it not. In a dream, in a vision of the night,
when deep sleep falleth upon men, in slumberings
upon the bed; Then he openeth the ears of men,
and sealeth their instruction, That he may with-
draw man from his purpose, and hide pride from
man. He keepeth back his soul from the pit, and his
life from perishing by the sword.   JOB 33:14–18

You spend approximately one third of your life
asleep. This is an inexorable law of life. This also
applies to the animal and vegetable kingdoms. Sleep
is a Divine ordinance, and many answers to our problems come to us when we are sound asleep upon the
bed.

Many people have advocated the theory that we
get tired during the day and that we go to sleep to rest

the body, and that a reparative process takes place while asleep. Nothing rests in sleep. Our hearts, lungs, and all the vital organs function. Our nails and our hair grow while asleep. If you eat prior to sleep, the food is digested and assimilated; also the skin secretes perspiration.

Dr. Bigelow, in his research work on sleep, demonstrated that in our dreams we receive impressions showing that the optic, olfactory, and gustatory nerves are active during sleep, and also the cerebral nerve centers are active. We must remember that there are qualities within us which never grow old, decay, or die. We cannot say that Love, Beauty, Peace, Joy, Patience, Veracity, Justice, Goodwill become fatigued or tired. Our body is composed of a confluence of atoms and molecules which comprise our cells, nerves, tissues, muscles, and bones. What we call matter is Invisible Energy reduced to the point of visibility; matter is characterized by inertia. It moves as it is moved upon. It acts as it is acted upon. The substance of your body is made of the same substance as the planets which have been dancing to the music of the spheres for myriads of years. The planets do not get tired or exhausted as they continue to move along their appointed orbits.

You go to sleep not just to rest your body, but to receive and participate in the Wisdom of God. Your conscious mind, busy in the workaday world, gets involved with the vexations, strife, and contentions of the day, and it is very necessary to withdraw periodically from sense evidence and the objective world and commune with the Indwelling God, thereby being replenished spiritually with wisdom, strength, and guidance enabling you to overcome all difficulties and solve your daily problems. Job reminds you that you may get answers to your problems in a dream and in a vision of the night.

Every night when you go to sleep you take your last waking concept with you into the deep where it is etched on the subconscious mind. In other words, the mood in which you go to sleep determines the experiences you shall have tomorrow, the next day, and the next, except you change your consciousness through prayer and meditation. Whatever you impress on your subconscious mind will be expressed as experience and events. Go to sleep every night feeling that your prayer is answered. Sleep brings counsel.

Dr. John Bigelow of England says, "No part of man's life deserves to be considered more indispensable to its symmetrical and perfect spiritual development than the whiles he is separated from the phenomenal world in sleep."

All of us know that in the sleep process our conscious mind is suspended temporarily, and we are sheltered from the distractions and fascinations of the phenomenal world, without which spiritual growth and development would be impossible.

The late Professor Agassiz, in one of his scientific works, relates a dream which solved his problem. He had been two weeks striving to decipher the somewhat obscure impression of a fossil fish on the stone slab in which it was preserved. Weary and perplexed, he puts his work aside at last, and tried to dismiss it from his mind. Shortly after, he awakened one night persuaded that while asleep he had seen his fish with all the missing features perfectly restored. But when he tried to hold and make fast the image it escaped him. Nevertheless, he went early to the Jardin des Plantes, thinking that on looking anew at the impression he should see something which would put him back on the track of his vision. In vain—the blurred record was as blank as ever. The next night he saw the fish again, but with no more satisfactory result. When he awoke, it disappeared from his memory as before. Hoping that the same experience might be repeated, on the third night he placed a pencil and paper beside his bed before going to sleep.

Accordingly, towards morning the fish reappeared in his dream, confusedly at first, but at last with such distinctness that he had no longer any doubt as to its zoological characteristics. Still half dreaming, and in perfect darkness, he traced these impressions on the sheet of paper at the bedside. In the morning he was surprised to see in his nocturnal sketch features which he thought it impossible for the fossil itself to reveal. He hastened to the Jardin des Plantes, and with his drawing as a guide, succeeded in chiselling away the surface of the stone under which portions of the fish proved to be hidden. When wholly exposed it corresponded with his dream and his drawing, and he succeeded in classifying it with ease.

If you are seeking an answer to a perplexing problem, cease maundering and asseverate quietly and firmly prior to sleep: "God knows the answer; I accept the answer now and give thanks."

You will recognize the answer by the inner silent knowing of your soul, by an inward sense of touch, or a spontaneous idea which may well up from your subliminal depths like toast pops up out of a toaster. When you talk to God, you expect an answer and you listen quietly, lovingly, and knowingly for Him. How can you hear if you refuse to listen? This is well expressed in Alfred Tennyson's "The Higher Pantheism."

"Speak to Him thou for He hears,
And Spirit with Spirit can meet—
Closer is He than breathing, and
Nearer than hands and feet."

The nature of Infinite Intelligence is responsiveness. It responds to you when you call upon It. Let me illustrate how the subconscious answers you. A young lady who comes to our Sunday morning lectures told me that she had been offered, a few months ago, a lucrative position in New York City at twice her present salary. She was wondering whether to accept or not and prayed as follows prior to sleep: "Father, thou knowest all things, reveal to me the right decision. Thank you for Thy guidance."

She repeated this simple prayer over and over again as a lullaby prior to sleep, and in the morning she had a persistent feeling that she should not accept the offer. She rejected the offer and subsequent events verified her inward sense of knowing, because the company went bankrupt in a few months following their offer of employment to her.

The conscious mind may be correct on the facts objectively known, but the intuitive faculty of the subconscious mind saw the failure of the concern in question and prompted her accordingly. We read in Acts 16:9 of instructions given to Paul when he was asleep. *And a vision appeared to Paul in the night; There stood a man of Macedonia and prayed him, saying, Come over into Macedonia and help us.* This changed the whole course of Paul's life.

During the month of May I gave a series of lectures in Town Hall, New York, under the aegis of the Church of Religious Science, New York. One night I had a dream in which a man said, "Get up and write this down, you are seeing my daughter Anna tomorrow." I awoke and went to the desk in the Algonquin Hotel and rustled through the drawer for a sheet of hotel stationery. He dictated to me as I wrote. I am sure that these instructions were not written by Joseph Murphy even half asleep, even by my subconscious in a half-dream world in which I was. I believe that it was the father of the girl whom I was to see the following day.

I definitely feel that it was the personality of her father, surviving so-called death, that gave me the instructions which explained in detail where a certain large sum of money was hidden, and also of holdings in the Bahamas with explicit instructions to his daughter whom to contact, etc., all of which was subsequently verified.

The following day Anna visited me at the Church of Religious Science Headquarters. I knew her because I had seen her in my dream the night previously. She knew me, and everything in the office was familiar to her. I believe that our dreams explain a great many of the statements and experiences of people who say,

"I've been here before." "I've seen him before." "I've heard that voice." "I have walked this path." There are times when a shining facet of our mind reflects the memories of things unseen objectively but seen subjectively, that which was not consciously known, but was subconsciously perceived and known. All of us dream, but we may not remember our dreams.

All prayer is a form of sleep whereby we become asleep to the world and its appearances and alive to the Presence and Power of God. Prayer means to withdraw and abstract your attention from the problem, difficulty, and evidence of senses, and focus your faith and confidence in God to guide, heal, and reveal the answer. In the prayer process you definitely reject the power of external conditions, and you affirm the supremacy and sovereignty of the Spirit within.

A young man had difficulty locating his father's will, and at night prior to sleep he prayed as follows: "Infinite Intelligence knows where the will is, and it is revealed to me now." He had a dream in which the location of the will was revealed to him.

In sleep there is a complete dissociation from the world in which we live, and our conscious attention to matters which engross our relations during the day are severed. Sleep is the inexorable master and is no respecter of persons. "The morning hour," says a German proverb, "has gold in its mouth."

If you have been upset, harassed, and worried during the day, and at night perhaps you read a psalm praying for peace, entering into the feeling of goodwill and the spirit of forgiveness to all, notice how you awake refreshed, with strength renewed, your mind serene and clear, your passions calmed, your animosities soothed, and kindlier feeling toward all.

The Bible says: *Remember the Sabbath day, to keep it holy.* Ex. 20:8. The Sabbath means rest in God, a stillness born of the conviction of the ever availability of the God-Presence at all times everywhere. We are in the Sabbath when we have complete trust and faith in God, knowing it is impossible for our prayer to fail. It is a feeling of inner certitude which follows true prayer.

Every night when you go to sleep feeling the joy of the answered prayer, you are in the Sabbath which means you have turned over your request to the Deeper Mind which is full of wisdom and intelligence. It knows the answer and will bring it to pass. There is always an interval of time between the impregnation of the subconscious and the external manifestation, and that is also called the Sabbath, or period of mental pregnancy.

When we are asleep the spiritual side of our life is in the ascendant. We are free from the world's hold upon our thoughts and feelings, and we are actually one with the Universal Life of God, and the Healing Currents of Eternity flow through our whole being while we are asleep.

The Mosaic Law set apart one day in seven for our spiritual reflection, and enjoined upon us to do no manner of work. It is for the same reason we are directed, when we pray, to enter into the inner chamber and shut the door, that we be not distracted by externals while we commune with our Father within. In sleep we are united by abstraction to our Higher Self, and we participate in His Healing Presence.

Yet the Lord will command his lovingkindness in the daytime, and in the night his song shall be with me . . . PSALM 42:8.

The processes of spiritual growth and development are more than ordinarily active during sleep. Job says that, while sleeping, God openeth the ears of men and sealeth their instruction. We are divinely instructed while asleep; moreover, whatever we take into the Deep as we go to sleep is etched in the subconscious mind which determines how it is to be expressed or made manifest. The many visions, prophetic dreams mentioned in the Bible were apparently given to the illumined men as they slept; perhaps because a Divine Truth was more sure of receiving attention and was less liable to encounter worldly obstruction and distractions during the sleeping than during the waking hours.

Sleep withdraws you from your purpose and hides pride from you, by showing you that while asleep, the whole world continues to function perfectly and that God is running the show.

He keepeth back his soul from the pit, and his life from perishing by the sword. JOB 33:18.

You can always avoid the pit of sorrow, grief, despondency, and the piercing sword of jealousy and anger by surrendering to God prior to sleep. Forgive everyone by pouring out God's love, peace, and joy upon them until there is no sting in your mind. Then talk to God, your Counselor and Guide, and affirm lovingly as you go off to the deep of sleep: "Father, thou knowest all things. Reveal to me the answer, heal me, guide me, comfort me, and let your river of peace flood my mind and heart."

Do this humbly and reverently every night, and you will never sit on a psychiatrist's couch, neither will you ever become neurotic, frustrated, or mentally deranged.

Lack of sleep can cause you to be irritable, moody, and depressed. Dr. George Stevenson of the National Association for Mental Health says, "I believe it can safely be said that all human beings need a minimum of six hours sleep to be healthy. Most people need more. Those who think they can get along on less are fooling themselves."

Medical research scholars investigating sleep processes and deprivation of sleep point out that severe insomnia has preceded psychotic breakdown in some instances. Remember, you are spiritually recharged during sleep, and adequate sleep is essential to producing joy and vitality in life.

Robert O'Brien, in an article, "Maybe You Need More Sleep" in an issue of "Reader's Digest" reports the following experiment on sleep:

"For the last three years experiments have been in progress at Walter Reed Army Institute of Research in Washington, D.C. Subjects—more than 100 military and civilian volunteers—have been kept awake for as long as four days. Thousands of tests have measured the effects on their behavior and personality. Results of these tests have given scientists astonishingly new insights into the mysteries of sleep.

"They now know that the tired brain apparently craves sleep so hungrily that it will sacrifice anything to get it. After only a few hours of sleep loss, fleeting stolen naps called 'lapses,' or micro-sleeps, occurred at the rate of three or four an hour. As in real sleep, eyelids drooped, heartbeat slowed. Each lapse lasted just a fraction of a second. Sometimes the lapses were periods of blankness; sometimes they were filled with images, wisps of dreams. As hours of sleep loss mounted, the lapses took place more often and lasted longer, perhaps two or three seconds. Even if the subjects had been piloting an airliner in a thunderstorm, they still couldn't have resisted micro-sleeps for those few priceless seconds. And it can happen to you, as many who have fallen asleep at the wheel of a car can testify.

"Another startling effect of sleep deprivation was its attack on human memory and perception. Many sleep-deprived subjects were unable to retain information long enough to relate it to the task they were supposed to perform. They were totally befuddled in situations requiring them to hold several factors in mind and act on them, as a pilot must when he skillfully integrates wind direction, air speed, altitude and glide path to make a safe landing."

Every night of your life, as you go to sleep, you are going before the King of Kings and the Lord of Lords, the Living Spirit Almighty. Be dressed for God mentally and emotionally. Go to sleep with the song of God in your heart, with love and goodwill for every living being in the world. Go into His presence clothed in the robes of love, peace, praise, and thanksgiving. You must be without spot or blemish when you visit God who is Absolute Love—the Immaculate Unblemished Presence. You must be all fair and no spot on thee. Wrap yourself in the mantle of Love, and go off to sleep with the praise of God forever on your lips.

You must remember there are many degrees of sleep, and every time you pray you are actually asleep to the world and alive to God. When you abstract your five senses from your problem or difficulty and focus all your attention on the solution or answer, knowing that the subjective wisdom of God is bringing about a solution in ways you know not of, you are practicing the art of sleep as mentioned in the Bible. You are asleep to the falsehood and hypnotic influence of the world when you accept as true what your reason and senses deny. When you hear of a person getting a nervous breakdown, you are reading of one who wandered away from God, and has cohabited mentally and emotionally with the false gods of fear, worry, ill will, resentment, remorse, and confusion.

Trustful relaxation is the remedy for insomnia. When you retire at night, let go of every worrisome and anxious thought. Cast out all burdens from the mind. Know that God is with you and that He has the answer. Abandon yourself to the thought that "underneath are the everlasting arms." Say over and over in quiet confidence: "I now relax and rest in God. I yield myself to God's river of peace. His peace and love pervade my whole being, and I sleep in peace. God giveth His beloved in sleep."

7

Not Resigned, But Reconciled

Troward says, "There are two ends to a stick." Emerson says, "We meet polarity or action and reaction in every part of nature." All of us know that our thoughts come in pairs. When you think of wealth, the thought of poverty comes into your mind also, and when you think of health, the thought of the opposite rears its head. Let us enumerate some of these opposites such as matter and spirit, negative and positive, darkness and light, evil and good, disease and health, pain and pleasure, misery and happiness, ebb and flow, male and female, in and out, subjective and objective, fear and love, heat and cold, rest and motion, yes and no.

The opposites are the expressions of the cosmos. They are dual expressions of the same principle. We are here to reconcile the opposites and bring harmony, health, and peace into our world. When it is cold you build a fire, when hungry you seek food, if sick you align yourself with the Healing Presence and establish wholeness and perfect health again. When fear strikes you, the thing to do is to mentally unite with the Source—God which is Love. You could read the 27th Psalm slowly, quietly, and lovingly, and as you do you are moving mentally to the opposite which is faith in God. Fear is a denial of the power of God and the goodness of God. Fear is faith upside down. Fear is a shadow in the mind, and there is no power in a shadow. "Perfect love casteth out fear." Fall in love with the good, become emotionally attached to the great truths of God, and all fear will go away.

If you are fearful, you can rest assured there is a desire within you for that which is opposite to the thing feared. Place your attention on the thing desired, and you will begin to reconcile the opposites. Desire is the angel of God, the messenger of the Divine saying to each one of us, "Come on up higher." Desire is behind all progress. Let your desire captivate and hold your attention. You move in the direction of the idea which dominates your mind. The greater the expected benefit from the desire, the stronger our desire.

I should like to tell you of a singer who failed to get a contract because his voice cracked on three occasions during an audition. Fear was his enemy, and he discovered he could move to the opposite which was faith and confidence through prayer. He stilled the wheels of his mind two or three times a day. He imagined he was singing before a microphone. He saw the imaginary audience. "Act as though I am, and I will be." He began to feel the joy of it all and the thrill of accomplishment. He continued to do this at regular intervals until he got the reaction which satisfied. He succeeded in planting his desire in his subconscious mind, and he felt a great sense of peace and satisfaction. He loved his desire to the point of acceptance and proved to himself that "perfect love casteth out fear."

Love is an emotional attachment, being loyal and devoted mentally to your ideal. As you do this the fear or the negative thought dies, and the ideal becomes real. This man is successful today because he learned how to reconcile the opposites in his life and bring peace where discord was. Give yourself wholeheartedly to your ideal, be loyal to it by mentally and emotionally uniting with it, you are loving it.

A soldier told me that he was cut off from his battalion in the last war and was in the midst of a hail of bullets. His knees were shaking with fear. He repeated the 23rd Psalm and a wave of peace came over him, and he found his way to safety. This soldier realized that if he remained at the extreme of fear he would be frozen to the spot, and the result would have been death and destruction. He let the pendulum of his mind swing to the opposite pole which was faith in God as his shepherd and protector from all harm.

The Bible says, *Ask, and it shall be given you; seek, and ye shall find; knock, and it shall be opened unto you; For every one that asketh receiveth; and he that seeketh findeth; and to him that knocketh it shall be opened. Or what man is there of you, whom if his son ask bread, will he give him a stone? Or if he ask a fish, will he give him a serpent? If ye then, being evil, know how to give good gifts unto your children, how much more shall your Father which is in heaven give good things to them that ask him?* MATTHEW 7:7–11.

These verses from the book of Matthew represent some of the greatest truths of the Bible, and set forth a wonderful formula for prayer. You are clearly told to ask, and you shall receive. To ask in Bible language is to claim your good, and then the Spirit within will honor and validate your claim. In these passages you are told God is your Heavenly Father, and you are to expect from Him all the blessings of Heaven. Look upon God as a loving father, a kindly father who watches over you, cares for you, guides and directs you, and provides for your welfare. As you make a habit of this you will discover that you will always be prospered, guided, and you will find yourself in your true place doing what you love to do, divinely happy, and divinely blessed in countless ways. God is to you what you conceive Him to be.

As long as man thinks that God is punishing him, testing him, or ruling over him with a rod of iron, a sort of jealous, cruel, or capricious tyrant, he will be confused, muddled, perplexed, and in mental conflict. Such thoughts being chaotic, the result is chaos and misery in his life. Man is what he thinks all day long.

Jesus states categorically, definitely, and unequivocally that God is our Father, and that we are His children. Your relationship with God should therefore be on the most friendly and loving terms, that of father and son. Never again during the whole course of your life look upon God as a God of wrath, indiscriminate in his vengeance. Such a concept held in the mind brings untold misery and suffering to the individual who entertains such a belief. Our beliefs are our masters, and all beliefs tend to manifest themselves in our lives.

Believe only that which is true of God; accept that which is lovely and of good report. Believe in the goodness of God, in the love of God, in the guidance of God, in the harmony of God, in the wisdom of the Almighty. Believe in the joy of God, and His abundance. Believe and expect all the blessings of Heaven here and now. According to your belief is it done unto you. Recognize the Fatherhood of God—God is your Loving Father; He loves you, and He cares for you. God wants you to be happy, joyous, and free. You are here to express the joy of living and to reproduce all the qualities, attributes, aspects and potencies of God.

I have said ye are gods, and all of you are sons of the Most High. It is fundamental and foundational to say that the offspring must be of the same nature and species of the parent. *I and my Father are one.* This means you and God are one mentally, spiritually, and physically. Infinity is within you, and therefore there is no end to the glory which is man. The journey is ever onward, upward, and Godward. You are capable of infinite growth and spiritual development.

Your greatest prayer is to still the wheels of your mind every morning, and for five or ten minutes feel that you are a channel through which God flows through you as harmony, health, peace, joy, wholeness, beauty, love, companionship, security, true place, and expression. Praying humbly and reverently in this manner you will expand in spiritual awareness until you have transcended even your fondest dreams.

Your glorious destiny is to be united with God and experience the glory which was yours before the world was. Cease being a serf, a slave, a doormat. Never say,

"I have to resign myself to my fate." "I must put up with this." "This is God's will and I must put up with my illness." "I'm incurable." "It's hopeless." "Etc." If you make such statements or have the mental attitude that you are here to suffer and that God is punishing you for your sins, you are placing yourself in thrall-dom, bondage, and degrading your Divine destiny as a son of the Living God here on earth to enjoy the inheritance of your Father.

Ask and ye shall receive is your passport and enfranchisement to freedom, health, supply, beauty, joy, and life more abundant. It could not be stated more emphatically or compellingly. It is absolutely wrong for you from every standpoint to remain in any kind of bondage whether physical, mental, or mate-rial. There is absolutely no virtue whatever in resigna-tion or being satisfied with your lot. To resign yourself to sickness or poverty is to sin or miss the mark of per-fect health and abundance. Resignation is a mixture of ignorance, fear, superstition, and indolence. Refuse to accept ill-health, discord, poverty, loneliness, or unhappiness.

God's beloved intention for you is the life more abundant, happiness, and peace of mind. You are here to let the Light of God shine in your mind, body, and environment. This is the only way you glorify God here and now. God is always successful in all

His undertakings. What is true of God is true of you because you are His son and heir to all His riches. It is your sacred task out of love for God to positively and definitely refuse to accept anything less than peace of mind, true place, abundance, and security. Keep on asking and knocking until the day breaks and the shadows flee away. *Knock and it shall be opened unto you.* This means that when you have a definite desire or idea in your conscious mind and have come to a clear-cut and definite decision in your conscious mind, you will then gain a response from your deeper mind which is full of wisdom and power. You refuse to take "no" for an answer because you believe implicitly in the promises of God: *Ask, and ye shall receive.* Keep on claiming your good continuously and untiringly until your prayer is answered.

A tragic and egregious blunder made by orthodox religious people is to think that the will of God for them is bound to be something tragic or evil or downright unpleasant. If the will of God for you were sickness, then all the doctors, psychologists, and nurses in the world would be working contrary to the will of God—this, of course, is the quintessence of absurdity. It is very unfortunate that millions of people look upon God as a hard, cruel, despotic taskmaster. Others believe in a devil that is tempting them. This belief in two powers results in endless confusion and a mental conflict accompanied by all kinds of strange fears and fixations.

Hear, O Israel, the Lord thy God is one Lord. There is only one Power which moves as a unity—this is a mathematical and spiritual necessity. Infinity cannot be divided or multiplied; there cannot be two powers, as one would cancel out the other, and there would be nothing but discord and chaos everywhere. Good and evil are the movements of our own mind relative to the One Being forever Holy, Pure, and Immaculate in Himself.

"I sent my soul into the Invisible, some letter of the after-life to spell. And bye and bye my soul returned to me, saying I myself am Heaven and Hell." The will of God is the nature of God. God is Life, and Life cannot wish death. God is Peace, and Peace cannot wish pain. God is Love, and Love cannot hate and build a fire where man burns for eternity.

There are many things God cannot do. He cannot violate His own Nature. Life cannot wish death, sickness, misfortune, or accident. We bring these things on ourselves by our own wrong thinking. Your heart would have to be full of hatred if you longed to see others suffer in a fire forever because they didn't belong to your creed or church, or because they erred and made serious mistakes. God is Love, and God is Absolute Harmony, and Harmony cannot wish discord. It is a fact that you can hate, but God is Love—that is the Truth which changes not, the same yesterday, today, and forever. It is a fact that you can create discord by misusing and misdirecting your subconscious mind, but the changeless Truth is that God is Absolute Harmony. It is a fact that you can lie, cheat, and defraud, but God is Absolute Truth, and the Universe is scrupulously honest, and God is Absolute Justice. There is a great difference between a fact and the Truth. The word fact comes from the Latin *factum,* your ability to create, manufacture in the factory of your mind.

You can use your mind two ways. Learn to use it the right way, and tune in on the Infinite Ocean of God's Love, Peace, Beauty, and Joy, and let these qualities flow through you. You do not create Harmony, Peace, Beauty, Joy, Love, or Health—you align yourself with these qualities of God by mentally tuning in with the Infinite, and letting His Splendor flow through you, in you, and all around you. The Will of God for you is greater freedom, greater self-expression, true place, perfect health, abundance, and blessings transcending your fondest hopes.

If you are a square peg in a round hole, and unhappy, you are not expressing the will of God. Inharmony and confusion will be the result. Resolve to express more and more of God's Love, and you will go from glory to glory. You and your desire are present now—these are the eternal two mentioned in the Bible. Your desire is whispering within you, and fear and doubt arise also. You must determine to resolve the quarrel in your mind so that peace is restored. Our early conditioning, fixed beliefs, and religious training impede and thwart our faith in God and all things good, and we find our mind is a battleground.

Your desire, as we said earlier, is of God and has its own mathematics and mechanics with it. Conditions, circumstances, and environment are not causative—these are effects and are subject to change. The fear thought that challenges your desire must die, and your desire must live. Take your attention completely away from the thought of opposition. This will starve it to death, and mentally and emotionally feast on your ideals. The latter is good, constructive, and wholesome, and will bless you. Your loyalty, devotion, and attention must be given to your goal, ideal, desire. Your thought-image is the first cause relative to the thing you are praying for, and is real on its own plane of reference.

Lift your mind and heart up beyond the problem or difficulty, and picture the fulfillment of your desire, the happy ending irrespective of opposition. Fear and false beliefs must die. Starve them to death by refusing them attention; give confidence and life to your ideal. This is the way of reconciling the opposites.

A famous space scientist, Dr. Von Blenk-Schmidt, who is doing research work on space travel, told me he is always running up against the devil, which simply means resistance, difficulties, and problems. Sometimes fear of failure enters in. He resolves these problems by prayer. He gets still and quiet and asks for the answer, and the creative ideas necessary for the solution come to him sometimes spontaneously out of the blue (the subconscious mind). Engineers, chemists, physicists working with him are trying to overcome atmospheric friction and resistance with various alloys of metals and new designs. There is always a way out, a solution, a happy ending. It is through difficulties and problems that we discover our Divinity. The joy is in the overcoming. If the crossword puzzle were all made out for you, life would be insipid, dull, and uninteresting.

You are here to discover your God-Self. If all your faculties functioned automatically, you could not discover your God-given powers and attributes. You can use your powers two ways, enabling you to deduce a law of life. Man is under the thralldom and bondage of the five senses until he awakens to the Creative Power of God. Realize your thoughts come in pairs. The fear thought is not real, it denies that which is actual. Be a spiritual paratrooper. Fly over the obstacle with the wings of faith and imagination, and feel, rejoice, and give thanks for the joy of the answered prayer.

Love is the fulfilling of the Law of Health, Happiness, Abundance, and Security. Wish for everyone what you wish for yourself, and fall in love with your ideal. Be faithful and loyal to your ideal, and it shall come to pass, and the Light of God will shine upon you.

8

The Master Secret Of The Ages

And the angel of the Lord appeared unto him in a flame of fire out of the midst of a bush: and he looked, and, behold, the bush burned with fire, and the bush was not consumed.

And Moses said, I will now turn aside, and see this great sight, why the bush is not burnt.

And when the Lord saw that he turned aside to see, God called unto him out of the midst of the bush and said, Moses, Moses. And he said, Here am I.

And he said, Draw not nigh hither: put off thy shoes from off thy feet, for the place whereon thou standest is holy ground.

EXODUS—CHAP. 3 VERSES 2–3–4–5.

And Moses said unto God, Behold, when I come unto the children of Israel, and shall say unto them, The God of your fathers hath sent me unto you; and they shall say to me, What is his name? what shall I say unto them?

> And God said unto Moses, I AM THAT I
> AM: *and he said Thus shalt thou say unto the chil-*
> *dren of Israel, I AM hath sent me.*
>
> Exodus—Chap. 3 Verses 13–14.

Man is looking everywhere for God, not know-ing that when he says "I Am" he is announcing the presence of the Living God within himself. This is called the master secret of the ages, sometimes referred to as the lost word. "I Am" means Being, Life, Aware-ness, The Presence of God in man. It is the nameless one.

In ancient times, the secret was given only to the initiated, never to the profane, because the ancient seers said with this knowledge, or awareness, a man can rise to the heights of spiritual illumination or he can sink to the depths of degradation. Hence, it was given only to those who were spiritually awakened and stood the tests that were given them.

This is how a woman applied the master secret in her own life. She attends my lectures at the Wilshire Ebell Theatre on Sunday and wrote as follows: "I am sixty five years old, a widow with a grown family. I am living alone and am on a pension. I heard you say one Sunday that whatever you attach to I Am, you become and if a woman is lonesome and wishes companionship that she should affirm with feeling 'I am wanted, I am happily married to a wonderful man and I am secure.' I began to affirm slowly, quietly, and lovingly, 'I am wanted, I am loved, I am happily married to a loving, kind and spiritual minded man. I am secure.' I kept on doing this every night and morning for about three weeks. A few days ago I went to the corner drug store. The druggist introduced me to a man who was a retired pharmacist. After a few days acquaintanceship he proposed to me and next month we are going on our honeymoon to Japan. He gave me a wedding present of $15,000."

Her prayer was felt as true in her heart and her affirmation sank down by osmosis into the subconscious mind, which is the creative medium. The moment she succeeded in bringing about a subjective embodiment, the subconscious brought about the answer through the law of attraction. The deeper mind full of wisdom and intelligence brought both of them together in Divine order.

Many are sound asleep because they do not know about this gold mine of Infinite Intelligence and Boundless Love within themselves. Whatever you want you can draw forth. A magnetized piece of steel will lift ten times its own weight. Demagnetize this piece of steel, and it will not even lift a feather. There are two types of men. There is the magnetized man who is full of confidence and faith in an Almighty Power to lead and guide him; he knows that he is born to win and to succeed. Therefore his deeper mind responds to Him. There is the other man who is demagnetized; he is full of fears and doubts. Opportunities come, and he says, "I might fail. I might lose all my money. People will laugh at me." This type of man will not get very far in life, because if he is afraid to go forward, he will simply stay where he is.

The magnetized man says, "I am going to succeed. The Power will back me up. I will prosper. There is nothing to stop me." The God Power moves through that man at his focal point of attention. Cease being demagnetized by doubts, fears, anxieties, and demoting yourself by saying, "I don't know the right people. I am too old. I haven't got the right politician," and so forth and so on.

The electrons, the atoms and the molecules are all the same in the magnetized and the demagnetized steel, but in the magnetized steel all the atoms and molecules are marshalled. They are focused in a certain direction. That is why it is a magnet. In the demagnetized steel, molecules move about at random and are not focused.

The ancients discovered that there was a Power with man, and that when man had confidence and faith in this Power, Lady Luck seemed to bless him in all his undertakings. When he was full of fear (of sickness for example that some germ would attack him), and he lived in that fear, he would create the disease. They realized that there was nothing external that could affect man except it affected him inside in his own mind. Nothing can touch you from the outside without your mental consent.

If you believe Lady Luck is with you, good fortune will smile on you. If you believe a jinx is following you, all kinds of trouble will come upon you. You begin to become suspicious of people and everything goes wrong and awry in your life because of your belief. Man's inner belief creates his personal good and evil. Man is belief expressed. The law of life is the law of belief. The Spirit within man is God. Spirit has no form, shape or substance. Spirit is timeless and ageless.

This unconditioned Being called God, becomes conditioned by conceiving Itself to be something. The whole world is simply this Being conceiving Itself to be all these things.

The whole world is a dramatization of God's ideas whether they are trees, suns, moons, stars, or continents. They are all God's ideas. God dramatizes Himself by conceiving and feeling Himself to be all these things. Everything in this world is alive, and the world that we see is not really solid at all. This is a world of intensities, frequencies, and densities, and the only difference between one substance and another is the number and rate of motion of the electrons revolving around a nucleus. The whole world is a world of vibrations.

The electron we speak of cannot be seen. The whole world is simply Spirit in differentiation. Matter is energy reduced to the point of visibility. Your thought is energy and it takes form. This is why thoughts are things. You are what you think all day long.

A little boy, fourteen years old, listens to my lectures on Sunday mornings. His father died some years ago and his mother couldn't afford a home. The little boy got a hammer, nails and some wood and built a miniature home. He put this small model on the mantlepiece of their home. The mother said, "What is that?" He said, "Mom, we want a home. If we look at this home, the picture of a new home will go into our subconscious." A man, for whom the boy works occasionally, donated him a home, so that he and his mother could live comfortably. This is the way the Law of Mind worked for this boy.

One day during the course of conversation, the man said, "Why don't you buy a home?" The boy said, "My mother hasn't the money." The man said, "I am going East to live with my son. I am not coming back to California any more. I have all the money I need. I have never done anything for anyone, but you are a nice boy and you deserve a break. You take this deed and give it to your mother." That is the way they got the home. The man never had seen the mother. He liked the boy and he gave them the home.

Strange? There is nothing strange about it. There are people in this country who give millions away.

He saith unto them, But whom say ye that I am? Who do you say this I AM within you is? What is your concept of God? What is your real belief? I am not talking about your intellectual assent. I am talking about your real belief, your deep functioning, abiding faith about this God-Power. Your concept, your blueprint and estimate of God is your whole concept of yourself, and your concept of yourself determines your entire future.

The answer you give to the question, *But who say ye that I Am?* determines your health, environment, social life, financial life, and all phases of your life, because your belief about God determines your whole life.

"I Am the Way." Yes, I Am is the Power that resurrects and makes alive the things that you are seeking, that which you want to be. This is the only Power and Presence, the only cause, the only Intelligence, the only Wisdom, the only Substance.

When you say, "I am poor," and so forth, you are making a poor mental arrangement in your own mind. Chant the beauty of the good and claim, "I am wealthy. I am happy. I am prosperous. I am healthy. I am secure. I am loved, I am illumined, and I am inspired." Watch the wonders in your life as you pray in this affirmative manner.

We have a new body every eleven months. Your thoughts are things and, as you fill your mind with the Truths of God, the electrons and the molecules of your body will undergo a transformation. There will be a dispersal of the old molecules, and the old electrons, which were diseased. "In my flesh shall I see God." You change your whole body through your thought and your feeling, and through your constant identification with the eternal verities.

There is no law compelling you to be depressed, dejected, vindictive, or to have destructive thoughts of poverty, lack and limitation.

You can be engulfed in the sea of despair, lack, ill will and gloom, because you have no inner bulwarks to man the ramparts. Learn where the God Presence is. Then you can say, "I am whole. I am watched over by the Love of God. I am surrounded by the whole armor of God and where I Am, God is." This attitude will render all your fears and doubts null and void. The waves of despair and despondency will go back to the seas, and you will walk over to dry land.

Your faith and confidence in God will lift you up and set you on the highroad to freedom, happiness, and peace of mind.

"I AM hath sent me unto you." Wouldn't it be wonderful if you went back to business tomorrow, to your factory, or to your conference and said, "God sent me here to solve all problems, to disperse anxiety, to bring peace where discord is, love where hatred is, joy where sadness is and to bring forth new ideas." Go forth with that attitude, and you can't fail. All the power and wisdom of God will flow through your focused point of attention—and this is called touching the hem of His garment.

The best way to realize your desire is to claim, feel and know that, "God gave me this ideal, this goal, this objective, and I am giving my attention and devotion to it now. I picture the end. I feel it and know that all the power of the Godhead is flowing through my mental image, and I am at peace."

There is an acid test for Truth. The fruits of Truth are joy, happiness, peace, love, goodwill, patience, and perfect health. This is the "Melody of God" which man plays. What good is any teaching, any religion?

What good is man himself except he becomes an instrument through which these Eternal Melodies are played.

The burning bush is within you, and you can lead your children (ideals, dreams and aspirations) out of Egypt, out of the darkness and into the Light of the Promised Land which means the realization of your desires. You are Moses, because you have the capacity to draw out the Wisdom and the Power that is within you.

Ye are the light of the world. This light is the Infinite Intelligence of God, that will illumine your pathway and will reveal to you everything you need to know. "A city that is set on a hill cannot be hid." You are the city of God, and all the thoughts and ideas in your mind are the people who live in this city.

If you are full of faith and confidence in God's Wisdom and believe with conviction that God will guide you, then that Light in you cannot be hid. Everyone will see it, because you are announcing the Presence and Power of God within yourself. You are announcing the presence of peace, of joy, of happiness.

The healing Rays of God flow through your eyes, your ears, and all your organs. You are suffused and submerged in the Holy Omnipresence and feel that God is vitalizing every cell and nerve of your body, so that your whole body dances to the rhythm of the Eternal God.

Feel a transfusion of God's grace flowing through you. Feel and know that this Holy Spirit which created you is now taking over all the processes and functions of your body.

"I Am the Way," "I Am the Truth," and "I Am the Life." "I Am the Door." Your own consciousness is the door to all expression, because what you claim and feel as true within yourself, the Spirit in you will honor, validate, execute and bring to pass. This is the way all things are made, and there is nothing made that is not made that way.

A wonderful sense of peace fills your soul. Let this Light of God be a torch to you. Lift up your eyes and behold that Light. Affirm, "God shows me the way. He is a lamp unto my feet; He is a light on my pathway." And that is exactly what God will be to you, because that which you believe God to be, He will be that to you. You live in the joyous expectancy of the best. His candle shines upon your head, and by His Light, you walk through darkness.

When the whole world says it can't be done, you will go inside, into the silence of your soul, and say, "It is done." You create the way God creates, by self contemplation of the Spirit, and what you conceive as true, you can give it conception.

I Am the way. Your own *I Amness* is the power that resurrects, that guides, that heals, makes alive whatever you feel to be true in your heart.

Your body is acted upon by the Creative Intelligence. You are Divine, you are Spiritual. You are joyous. You are surrounded by the Peace of God. The Spirit of God pervades every atom of your being, your children, your home, your business. There is Divine Right action in your life. You are instantaneously healed by the Presence and Power of the Almighty.

There is Divine equilibrium in your body, which you sense and feel, and you rejoice that there is but One Presence and One Power and It is moving as a unity and as a harmony through you. You live, move, act, and have your being in God. You feel that it is impossible for your prayer to fail. The answer comes to pass in due season, in God's own way, and in God's own time, for God is bringing it to pass now in His own way.

When fear or worry comes into your mind, you do not entertain these thoughts. You chant the Beauty of the Good, and affirm, "God is guiding me now. God is taking care of me, and all is well. The Creative Intelligence of God, which is regnant and supreme, brings all my requests to pass in Divine Order. According to my faith is it done unto me. It is wonderful!"

9

You Are What You Eat

These are the beasts which ye shall eat; the ox, the sheep, and the goat.

The hart, and the roebuck, and the fallow deer, and the wild goat, and the pygarg, and the wild ox, and the chamois.

And every beast that parteth the hoof, and cleaveth the cleft into two claws, and cheweth the cud among the beasts, that ye shall eat.

Nevertheless these ye shall not eat of them that chew the cud, or of them that divide the cloven hoof; as the camel, and the hare, and the coney: for they chew the cud, but divide not the hoof; therefore they are unclean unto you.

And the swine, because it divideth the hoof, yet cheweth not the cud, it is unclean unto you: ye shall not eat of their flesh, nor touch their carcase.

These ye shall eat of all that are in the waters; all that have fins and scales shall ye eat:

And whatsoever hath not fins and scales ye may not eat; it is unclean unto you.

Of all clean birds ye shall eat.

But these are they of which ye shall not eat: the eagle, and the ossifrage, and the ospray.

And the glede, and the kite, and the vulture after his kind, And every raven after his kind,

And the owl, and the night hawk, and the cuckow, and the hawk after his kind,

And the little owl, and the great owl, and the swan, And the pelican, and the gier eagle, and the cormorant,

And the stork, and the heron after her kind, and the lapwing, and the bat.

And every creeping thing that flieth is unclean unto you: they shall not be eaten.

But of all the clean fowls ye may eat.

Ye shall not eat of any thing that dieth of itself: thou shalt give it unto the stranger that is in thy gates, that he may eat it; or thou mayest sell it unto an alien: for thou art an holy people unto the Lord thy God. Thou shalt not seethe a kid in his mother's milk.

DEUT. CHAP. 14:4–21

All of us have heard the expression, "You are what you eat." If a thing is true, there is a way in which it is true. There is a way in which the verses in the fourteenth chapter of Deuteronomy are true. They are true psychologically and spiritually and represent many of the most profound truths in the entire Bible.

The Bible is a textbook on psychology and the science of living and it cannot be taken literally. The spiritual key to the Bible does away with all superstitions, literalisms and rescues us from all the seeming contradictions, inconsistencies and historical dilemmas. Except we have the inner meaning of the Bible, we really do not have any Bible.

I have known people who have had the choicest food and a perfectly balanced diet, according to the laws of nutrition, and yet they developed ulcers, cancer and other destructive and degenerative diseases. The food we eat is transmuted by the Creative Intelligence within us into tissue, muscle, bone, blood, hair, etc.

If we are hateful, envious, jealous and full of hostility, the food we eat may well be transformed into various diseases of a psychomatic nature. Our moods and attitudes of mind determine whether our food will build health or disease. If we are full of good-will and eat our food with joy and thanksgiving, it will be transmuted into beauty, vitality, wholeness and strength. The bread or meat which you eat, after a few hours, becomes your flesh and blood. This is essentially the doctrine of transubstantiation, when shorn of its superficial wrappings and trappings.

Food for the body is very important. Today some of our foremost research physicians are pointing out the dangers of excessive fat which interferes with the mechanical efficiency of all our vital organs, such as the heart, lungs, liver, and kidneys. We know that many physical and mental diseases can result from lack of certain vitamins and chemicals. Beriberi, a disease characterized by multiple inflammatory changes in the nerves, producing great muscular debility, is brought about by insufficiency of vitamin B. Research experiments on animals depriving them of manganese and other elements bring on mental and physical deterioration and degeneration. We are all familiar with the necessity of sufficient calcium for the pregnant mother. Deficiency of Vitamin A has deleterious effects on the eyes and a sufficient amount of protein is essential for our well being. All this is most important, but our own mental and spiritual diet is of the greatest importance.

The Bible says, *Thou shalt not eat any abominable thing,* which means that you should not entertain or enthrone in your mind negative thoughts such as resentment, ill will, cynicism, hate or anger. Animals in the Bible represent animated states of consciousness. Emotions follow your thoughts. If you think hateful thoughts, you will generate a destructive emotion, which is one of the animals you should not eat of. Emerson said, "You are what you think all day long." The Bible says: *As a man thinketh in his heart so is he.* Distinguished research physicians and other scientists point out that we have a new body every eleven months. You are creating new cells all the time, and if you fill your mind with the eternal verities and spiritual values of life, your brain will send these spiritual vibrations through the medium of your nervous system all over your body, and all the new cells will take on the vibration of these spiritual overtones, so that, like Job, you will be able to say: *Yet in my flesh shall I see God.*

You are eating of the truths of God when you mentally and emotionally dwell on whatsoever things are just, honest, lovely, and of good report.

Eating in Biblical language refers to our mental and spiritual diet. We are fed daily through the five senses by an avalanche of sights, sounds, sundry concepts—good and bad, but most of this food is highly unsavory. We must learn to turn inward to God and be replenished from the standpoint of Truth. For example, affirm frequently—with feeling, "God is guiding me now, God's Love fills my soul, God inspires me, God's river of peace floods my mind and heart. I hear the Truth, I love the Truth and I radiate love and goodwill to all." This prayer is wonderful spiritual food for your mind. You will find yourself guided in all your ways and that will also refer to the food you select because the Nature of Infinite Intelligence is responsiveness and It responds to the nature of your thought.

You are told you may eat the beasts that parteth the hoof and cleaveth the cleft into two claws, and cheweth the cud such as the cow, the sheep, the goat, etc.

The hoof is a wonderful symbol which means understanding, our capacity to choose, divide and select. The Bible says, *Choose ye this day whom ye shall serve.* Choose the concepts and ideas which are true. Use your reasoning faculty to discern and discriminate between what is true and false. When you learn to choose correctly, you will no longer choose sickness, accident, poverty, pain, misery or lack. You may eat of the choicest food and be hungry in your heart for peace, joy, love, happiness, and inspiration. Every day of your life, mentally eat of God's ideas of wisdom, truth, and beauty. You choose the bread of Heaven whenever you turn away from the world and sense-evidence, and mentally feast on the Truth that there is only One Power operating through the thoughts, feelings and imagery of your mind.

When you read the newspapers, listen to the radio and press reports, you read of suffering, war, injustice, crime, poverty, and lack of all kinds. Shakespeare said, "Man's inhumanity to man makes countless thousands mourn." You may feel the strains and stresses of your business or profession. Perhaps the vexations, arguments and difficulties of the day have unduly upset you. If so, divide the hoof and chew the cud. You must choose the Truth and chew on it in the sense that you appropriate it by meditating on it and absorbing it until the true ideas become a part of you in the same way that a glass of milk becomes your blood stream. You must meditate on the Truths of God until you feel radiant, happy, and free, then you are one with God and you feel His Presence in your whole being. To divide the hoof is to arrive at the Truth in your mind, and see the spiritual values which never change and are the same yesterday, today, and forever. However, this is not enough, you must now chew the cud like a cow. The cow has several stomachs. She feeds on the grass, passes it from one stomach to another and when she feels contented, she lies down on the field and chews the cud. This is a process whereby she brings the food previously absorbed into her mouth as a sort of bolus, and begins to masticate it all over again until the food is thoroughly digested and appropriated completely by the whole system. You chew the cud by mentally dwelling on God's Wholeness, Perfection, Power and Wisdom until your mind is lifted up and exalted. As you do this, your mind will be fascinated, engrossed, and absorbed in the great Truths you are feasting on. You will hunger no more, nor thirst any more, for God in His Wisdom becomes a lamp unto your feet and a light on your path.

The swine divideth the hoof, yet cheweth not the cud and is called unclean. The reason for this is obvious to you by now. Many people have a wonderful intellectual grasp of the Truth. They accept the Truth readily with the conscious mind only. Intellectual assent to the Truth is not enough. There are people who agree that honesty is the best policy, but they don't always practice it. Millions perhaps give lip service to the Ten Commandments, but these are constantly broken. When these Truths are accepted by the subconscious mind, and thus assimilated into the whole mentality, a tremendous difference takes place in one's character or life. You can taste clover in the milk of the cow after she has chewed the cud, the reason being, she has appropriated, assimilated and digested the clover so thoroughly that she exudes the aroma in the milk, which is a part of her. Likewise, when you appropriate, meditate and feast on the qualities, attributes and potencies of God you will be under a Divine compulsion to express these qualities as they become a part of your nature. The swine divides the hoof and chews not the cud; it is therefore unclean. There are people who write and talk glibly on how to use the Healing Power of God, yet many live in an unhealthy way, notwithstanding. Many philosophers who write on the wisdom of the ages, and give intellectual assent to the same are extremely unhappy, frustrated and neurotic. I knew a man who wrote a wonderful book on nutrition; it was quite scientific and very sound. He had acute ulcers and was most unhappy. He had head knowledge and failed to let it become heart knowledge. He failed to meditate, reflect and mentally digest what he wrote so that it would be incorporated into his subconscious. He would then have followed his own physical diet as well as the mental and spiritual vitamins which he also recommended. The truths of God must be appropriated and impressed into the subconscious, before a real change takes place.

You should not eat of the camel, and the hare, and the coney because they chew the cud and divide not the hoof. There are people who dream about a state and never appropriate it. I have talked to people in England and Ireland and other countries, who suffered from various ailments, such as rheumatism, sciatica, asthma, hay fever, etc. I talked to them about the Healing Presence and the scientific work being done in the psychosomatic field of medicine which listed the mental and emotional factors behind their ailments. They agreed with me and said it was interesting and undoubtedly true, but they did nothing about it. They refused to divide the hoof, and come to a clear-cut decision, that they could be healed and according to their decision would it be done unto them. The moment you come to a clear-cut, definite decision in your conscious mind, that you can be healed, your Deeper Mind which is full of Wisdom and Intelligence will respond accordingly. They refused to change their consciousness and consequently remained as they were. There is the man who is always *talking* about the book he is going to write, the new business he is going to open up. He never does anything—it's all talk. He lacks decision, judgment, and discrimination.

There are a great number of people who chew the cud in this way. They study the various religions of the world, they read a vast number of inspirational books, they study numerology, astrology, various philosophies and become charter members of every new and strange cult. They become muddled, perplexed and so confused that many of them become mentally and emotionally disoriented and unbalanced. You must divide the hoof by deciding once and for all what the Truth is and build your whole life on that impregnable rock which never changes.

You divide the hoof by selecting what is eternally true, and all your reading, thought, instruction, and decisions must meet and conform to the following standard: *Whatsoever things are just, whatsoever things are pure, whatsoever things are lovely, whatsoever things are of good report; if there be any virtue, and if there be any praise, think on these things.* PHIL. 4–8.

This is the master spiritual standard which enables you to choose what is noble and God-like for the sanctuary of your own mind. Anything and everything that does not conform to this spiritual standard must positively and definitely be rejected as unfit for the house of God, which is your mind.

All fish that have fins and scales, ye can eat, the meaning of which is quite apparent. Scales represent the armor of God which Paul speaks of. *And the Lord, He it is that doth go before thee.* Your conviction of God's Presence is a mighty armor of protection, which goes before you, making straight, beautiful, joyous, and happy your way. All the highways and byways of your world are controlled by God, making the skies above and the earth beneath a highway for your God. The fish with fins have the power of propulsion and they steer themselves. All of us know the story of the salmon. Driven by inner wisdom he makes his way back across the ocean, overcoming all hurdles and obstacles to the place of his birth, where he dies, bequeathing his life forces to other forms of himself.

Man has fins and scales when he knows that he can choose, direct, and control his own destiny. His thought and feeling control his destiny. Man who does not choose his own thought and fails to meditate on the eternal verities becomes a victim of the race mind and moves along with the flotsam and jetsam of life, becoming subject to all the trials and tribulations of the race mind. If man does not do his own thinking, the race mind, the newspaper, the columnists and the newscasters and his relatives will do his thinking for him. Fish without fins and scales are at the mercy of the tides and are cast upon the beach to die. Cease drifting, steer your ship. Let God lead and guide you. Choose health, choose prosperity. Choose success. Let God lead and be your Silent partner in all your undertakings.

You are a conqueror. The world is not your master. Conditions and circumstances are effects, not causes. Your mind and Spirit are cause. You can change conditions. You are not subject to the political tide, the financial tide or the tide of national events. Identify with your goal, image it, feel it, and know the Almighty Power of God is moving on your behalf. As you continue to nourish your ideal with faith and confidence, you will experience the joy of the answered prayer. There is nothing to oppose Infinite Intelligence. It is All-Powerful, The Ever-living One, the All-Knowing One and the All Powerful One.

You shall not eat the vulture, the raven or the hawk for the simple reason that they are birds of prey. You must not take advantage of others by preying on their weaknesses, lack of understanding and ignorance. Some men pray together on Sunday and prey on each other on Monday. The vulture hovers overhead to eat the dead carcass. Like many other birds it is a scavenger. Men are scavengers when they feed on grudges, peeves, ill-will, hatred and resentment. Love, peace, joy, beauty, happiness, vitality and strength die in us when we eat mentally of these destructive states.

We must not eat the cuckow, because this bird is noted for the habit of laying its eggs in the nests of other birds for them to hatch, instead of building a nest of its own.

Do not have the characteristics or habits of the cuckow. Learn to lean on God, not on others. Stand on your own feet, don't expect others to do all the work for you. You are here to put your shoulders to the wheel, also. You have responsibilities, you have oars in the way of two hands, and a brain also, and you must pull your share. You are a Son of God on a voyage of self-discovery, and you must learn to build your own nest and draw forth the gifts and powers of God within you. You are prohibited from eating the raven, because it is omnivorous and predaceous. If you rob, cheat, or defraud others, this will react on yourself, resulting in loss of health, wealth and peace of mind. To hurt another is to hurt yourself. Birds have two wings; likewise we have two wings, namely, thought and feeling. If you think evil of another and your mind being creative, will create what you think, thereby polluting your own soul.

Every creeping thing that flieth is unclean. This means that man must cease thinking of himself as a worm of the dust, apologizing for being alive and judging everything according to appearances. We can fly in our imagination to any heights or depths. Imagination is the workshop of God, but many misuse, distort and diabolically pervert this God-given faculty. Imagination enables us to soar aloft above the storms and stresses of life and see and feel the happy ending, the Divine solution, the answered prayer.

I shall illustrate this by telling you about a man who crawled along the ground in the mud and mire of fear, hatred, and ill will. His wings were clipped, and he ceased to move onward, upward, and Godward. He had been smarting from a letter received from his general manager. His attitude was, "This is the last straw—this I can't take." He was boiling and seething with resentment, saying to himself, "This I can't forgive after all my years of faithful service, etc."

He was crawling in the mire of resentment and revenge. At my suggestion, he used his wings and imagination the right way. Every night before he went to sleep, he sat humbly down imagining the general manager had written him a letter which praised him and his work, and which satisfied him in every way according to the Golden Rule, the Law of Love and Good-will. He saw the words in the imaginary letter. He rejoiced in reading them. He said to me, "I kept it up every night. I would read that letter over and over again and look at the general manager's signature." All hatred left him as he continued to do this. To quote him again, "The queerest thing in all the world happened!" The general manager wrote him a letter praising and promoting him. The letter was the essence of what he had been imagining and feeling for several days.

Every creeping thing that flieth is unclean—the man no longer used his imagination from a creeping, crawling, muddy standpoint, but with the wings of faith and imagination, he pictured conditions as they ought to be. He substituted the mood of love and good-will for the feeling of ill will and hostility. Orage, a student of Ouspensky, used to give a wonderful technique for solving personal problems as follows: "Compose a letter, written as from your friend to yourself, which would completely satisfy you if you received it. Put into it such words as you would like your friend to do or write to you." The above mentioned young man rejoiced in reading the contents of the imaginary letter, and the All Wise-Deeper Self cast the spell of God around the general manager, causing him to respond in kind. Give love and you will receive love.

Ye shall not eat of anything that dieth of its self.

Thou shalt not seethe a kid in its mother's milk.

We should always eat of the nourishing truths of God which live forever and never die. Fear, hate, jealousy, condemnation, revenge, ill will, etc., should die in us. We should take our attention away from all negative states and feast on goodness, truth and beauty all the days of our lives. Opinions, theories, creed, dogmas, philosophies, conditions, circumstances pass away—they die of themselves. Do not eat of these things which undergo change and decay but meditate on God's eternal Love, Light, Truth and Beauty, which are the same yesterday, today and forever. "Change and decay, all around I see, O Thou who changeth not abide with me!" All things in this world pass away. Dwell on the great truths of life which never pass away and you will become what you contemplate.

You shall not seethe a kid in his mother's milk. Many people will not drink milk with meat, as they take the Bible literally. A kid is a symbol of sacrifice. Milk is a universal food, a symbol of nourishment. Do not nourish a grudge or dwell on resentment. If you do, you are giving attention to the kid and you will become the goat. Whatever you give your attention to magnifies and grows in your experience. You should sacrifice the kid (grudge, hate, etc.), by consuming it in the fire of Divine Love, for your God is a consuming fire. Radiate love, peace, joy and goodwill to the other until all the roots of ill-will are burned up. If you nurse the grudge and emotionalize it (mother's milk), you may develop tumors, growths, and other discordant bodily states, causing you to become the goat. (You don't really want to ride the goat).

Watch your mental and emotional diet. Divide the hoof by choosing what is true, noble, and God-like. Choose your thoughts from the standpoint of God and hang the walls of your mind with pictures of whatsoever things are lovely, and of good report. Choose the mood of faith, expecting the best, and fill your mind with God's Love. Chew the cud morning, noon, and night by lighting the fire of Divine Love in your heart, which will keep you warm and cheerful at all times. Absorb the truths of Life, let them saturate and gestate in your soul and you will become like a tree planted by the rivers of water, and whatever you do will prosper.

Go thy way and eat thy food with joy and let the joy of the Lord be your strength now and forevermore.

10

The Magic Quality of Self-Confidence

Now faith is the substance of things hoped for, the evidence of things not seen. For by it the elders obtained a good report. Through faith we understand that the worlds were framed by the word of God, so that things which are seen were not made of things which do appear. But without faith it is impossible to please him: for he that cometh to God must believe that he is, and that he is a rewarder of them that diligently seek him.

HEBREWS 11:1, 2, 3, 6.

The eleventh chapter of Hebrews is the greatest chapter in the Bible on building self-confidence. Confidence means *with faith*. Faith is an awareness of the presence and power of God within you.

Man may have confidence in stocks, bonds, real estate, in his ancestors, academic distinction, and perhaps in his qualifications, etc., all of which is good in its own way, but all these things pass away and are not stable. Man must have confidence in the Principle of Life which responds to his thought and never fails him.

Many people have faith in a system of theology, in certain ecclesiastical dogmas, but they have no working faith at all, and their lives are chaotic. Others who have a system of theology have a workable faith. They express it in their business, in their talents, in their homes, and in their relationship with people.

Confidence gives you a light in your eye, a new stance, and a fresh grip on life. You wear a smile. You are filled with vitality and energy. A person reflects his confidence in himself by his posture, manners, gestures, speech, and by the look in his eyes. Every part of him reveals his estimate or blueprint of himself. In that way many people can read character by watching a person walk. Others can read character by listening to a man talk. This is why psychologists and psychiatrists listen to their clients, who reveal themselves in their speech and in the timbre and tone of their voice.

Approve of yourself and have a high estimate of yourself because you are an individualized expression of God. You are a son or expression of the Living God. Adopt this attitude of mind, and you will lose the sense of inferiority. I know people whose faith seems to be in the money they can make in the stock market; but the stock market rises and falls. Your faith must be in that which never changes, namely the spiritual values of life, the laws of your mind, and the Principle of Life which remains the same yesterday, today, and forever. Theologies, philosophies, governmental operations, fiscal values, etc., wax and wane, come and go. Governments topple, wars and strife cause money to lose its value. Sometimes floods, hurricanes, and other cataclysms of nature sweep cities, towns, and homes away. Everything in this world passes away and is subject to change. *Change and decay all around I see. Oh, Thou who changeth not abide with me.*

To really acquire self-confidence, you must have faith in the Eternal Principle of Life within you which created you and also the world. You must by study and application develop confidence in the two phases or functions of your mind, namely the conscious and subconscious. The subconscious mind responds to your habitual thinking. You can choose your thoughts, imagery, reactions, and response to life. You can channel your emotions constructively. You can develop confidence in the subconscious mind in the same way you would have confidence in chemistry, physics, mathematics, or electronics in building a radio or television set. A doctor has confidence when he begins to operate, because he knows surgery, anatomy, physiology, and other basic sciences dealing with the human body.

Many people say, "I am shy; I am timid; I am no good; I am abashed; I was born on the wrong side of the tracks; I did not have a good education; I did not go to college." All these negative thoughts pass through the minds of people then comes self-protection. Some retreat into themselves saying, "I want to be alone." They shun company and become self-centered, and their mentalities become warped. They are afraid of getting hurt, so they will not go to other people's homes or to a local party, lest their psychic boil get hurt.

This attitude of mind is due to a sense of rejection, which is primarily due to the fact they have no confidence in the God-Self within. Furthermore, many of these psychic traumas go back to childhood, when the parents may have said, "You are no good, you will never amount to anything. You will be a drunkard like your father, etc." The way to overcome all sense of inferiority and rejection is to realize that you can change your concept of yourself, and that conditions, circumstances, and events are not causative, these are effects. The basic cause of all fear is to believe that externals are causative. The cause of all is your own mind and spirit.

The Bible says, *If God be for me, who can be against me?* Take this statement of Truth and feel that the

God-Presence is flowing through you as strength, beauty, love, peace, security, and true place. Realize that you are one with God, and that as you think of harmony, health, peace, joy, power, and happiness, the God-Presence responds, bringing all these qualities to pass in your life. As the God-Presence flows through these patterns of thought, you become creative, and you become what you want to be, to do, and to have, irrespective of what other people say, do, or think.

You can banish all sense of inferiority by affirming, feeling, and knowing the truths in the following prayer: "I am a channel for God's Life, Love, Truth, and Beauty. I am an expression of God. God is my Father. God loves me and cares for me. I am a unique expression of God, and there is no one in all the world like me. God seeks to express Himself in a unique and extraordinary way through me. I am a pipeline for His power and strength, and every day of my life I am expressing more and more of my hidden power. I radiate love and goodwill to all, and I wish for everyone what I wish for myself. I am one with my Father, and my Father is God."

Dwell on the above truths several times a day and particularly prior to sleep at night, and you will find all sense of inferiority and rejection disappear. Remember that when you give life-giving thoughts and new mental patterns to your subconscious mind, the latter accepts the new imagery, and the past is obliterated and expunged from the subconscious mind. Prayer changes the subconscious mind by eliminating all the subjective patterns which were causing all the trouble. Prayer is filling your mind with the truths of God, thereby crowding out of the mind everything unlike God, or the Truth.

The late Henry Hamblin, editor of the Science of Thought Review, London, England, told me that one Sunday morning he received a call from the local Congregational minister. This was when he first started to write along spiritual lines. The minister wanted him to deputize for him that morning. He had never conducted a Congregational service, and did not know the routine or procedure. He said that he was panic stricken, filled with consternation, foreboding, and cold shivers ran down his spine. He began to ask himself, "Where is my confidence? Where is my faith in the things that are right?" There was no time to open the Bible or to prepare a sermon. He walked onto the podium, and the people began to sing their hymns, and entered into their thanksgiving prayer.

He began to say to himself, "God guides and reveals to me what to say." Suddenly, the quotation, *Turn your eyes unto the hills from whence cometh your help,* came to him, and he mentally surrendered affirming, "I surrender, God takes over and speaks through me."

Instantaneously the burden of fear was dissipated. He was lifted up by the Spirit so that he saw intuitively into the hearts of all the people present. He saw them struggling, striving, scrambling, squabbling for the baubles of life. They did not seem to know where they were going. He said that he apparently saw into the hearts of all humanity.

This was a cosmic vision given to him by the Spirit. He saw people's hopes, fears, their loves and hates, their joy, frailties, their shortcomings, and their derelictions—all simultaneously. A divine compassion for them seized him. Just as suddenly as it came, the vision vanished, and he began to talk, and the entire congregation was held spell-bound. They were seized and imbued by the Holy Spirit. It was his recognition of the Spirit within which gave him the confidence he needed. All members of the audience felt the intangible, invisible spiritual overtones which permeated them subjectively. He discovered the Power that moves the world and which answers when called upon. This is the way to build up self-confidence.

But without faith it is impossible to please Him: for he that cometh to God must first believe that He is, and that he is a rewarder of them that diligently seek Him.

When you turn to God, God turns to you. His nature is responsiveness, and you are rewarded according to the nature of your thought and the measure of your acceptance. A young man, who listens to the writer on the radio in the mornings, wrote me saying that he was too shy and timid to propose to his girl, and that every time he tried, he became tongue-tied and panic stricken. Fear held him in bondage.

In talking to him I suggested that every night prior to sleep he imagine he is acting the way he desires to act when in the presence of the girl. He pictured himself as the ardent lover and said, "This is the way I am proposing to her now." He would dramatize the imaginary act over and over again every night. He made this mental movie as vivid as possible. He emphasized that he would actually behave that way and that he was completely calm and poised. On the twentieth evening he went to her home and with faith, fervor, and confidence proposed and was accepted.

Too many people have a churlish timidity toward life. Put on the whole armor of God by knowing that God thinks, speaks, and acts through you. If you feel inferior in the face of a dilemma, some perplexing situation, or certain assignment, begin to think of all the reasons why you can overcome, achieve, and arrive at a happy solution. Say to yourself, "I shall conquer through the Power of the Almighty." All of us know that Abraham Lincoln felt inferior to the task assigned to him of making a speech commemorating the battle of Gettysburg. He prayed for guidance, studied parts of the Bible, and asked God to give him counsel and strength. He approached the subject with humility, simplicity, and with a deep reverence for things Divine. *He that cometh to God must believe that He is, and that he is a rewarder* . . . Lincoln believed that God always answered prayer. His simplicity, devotion to Truth, and humility before God caused him to produce the greatest address in history.

When you face a difficult problem, become aware of the Divinity within and say to yourself, "This problem is divinely outmatched because I see God, and whatever is necessary for me to know and to do, God reveals it to me." Go ahead and tackle the situation doing the best you can, and you will find Infinite Spirit will aid and assist you. The dawn will appear, and all the shadows will flee away.

Do not waste your energy. Watch the expenditure of your thought by saying to it that all your thoughts are invested wisely. Remember that the law of parsimony must prevail in your mind, and you must economize in your mental assumptions. You must assume that God is and that He answers you. *Faith is the substance of things hoped for* . . . Faith is to perceive the reality of the idea, thought, or image in your mind. You have faith when you know that the idea of a book, play, composition, or invention in your mind is as real as your hand or heart. This is the substance of things hoped; this is the evidence of things not seen. I do not see the new invention in your mind, but as you accept it and give it attention, the law of growth will take place. Like the seed in the ground, you will attract everything necessary for its unfoldment. What you give attention to you will experience.

It is very strange how people expect to get ahead in life, be happy and healthy without organizing their mental faculties, or even knowing anything about them. You would not operate an automobile if you had no experience, neither would you operate a chemical laboratory if you knew nothing about chemistry. Thinking is a process as real and as definite as the making of sodium hydroxide or bicarbonate of soda. You think with your own mind, and you can make wonderful mental combinations which will transform your life. Thoughts are things, and as a man thinketh in his heart, so is he.

To worry is to deflect your attention deliberately away from the good and to mentally focus on the negative aspects of life. Your thoughts go round and round as you dizzily seek a way out of the dilemma. Come back from the periphery to the center, where God abides, and find the answer within.

When we attempt mental imagery we must feel the picture. There must be an emotional tone to vitalize it. The pictured scene is a dramatization, a series of mental patterns, which you feel as true. The majority of people go to business and other activities with the wrong mental imagery, bringing about all kinds of trouble in their lives. Their minds are naked. Your mind must be clothed with faith in God and all things good. You must believe in the goodness of God and in the guidance of God, and in His Overshadowing Presence at all times. When your mind is thus clothed, you are wearing the garments of God. You would not go in sport clothes to a presidential banquet, nor would you wear evening clothes in the swimming pool. Are you dressed mentally for God, or is your mind full of rags, and of torn and tattered garments? You must wear psychic clothing for all occasions. When going on a journey know that, "Divine Love goes before me, making straight, beautiful, and joyous my way."

The Bible states clearly that if you wear the mental garment of faith that you will be *like the men who through faith subdued kingdoms, wrought righteousness, obtained promises, stopped the mouth of lions, quenched the violence of fire, escaped the edge of the sword, out of weakness were made strong, waxed valiant in fight, turned to flight the armies of aliens.* HEBREWS 11:33–34.

These are the wonderful things, which confidence in God accomplishes. You actually find that, as you build up your awareness of the Power of God in your mind, all the so-called insuperable obstacles are overcome by you. There are people who have escaped fires, floods, hurricanes, disasters at sea, subdued lions, and the ravages of war. Nothing touched them; they seemed to lead charmed lives. The spell of God was around them. They were God intoxicated, having acknowledged and received the Divine Antibody, the Presence of God in the midst of them, mighty to heal, save, and protect.

William James said, "Believe in the good life, and believe that Life is worth living, and your belief will cause this to become a fact."

Cease identifying with failure, lack, and limitation. Unite with your goals and aspirations. Timidity is a state of mind. The timid are usually consummate egotists who try to hide their blatancy in mental retreat. The timid must do the things that they fear to do, and the death of fear is certain. We have to win with pleasure in the game of life and lose with a smile.

Demosthenes stuttered badly. He decided to become a great orator, and he persevered until he won the battle. Victory was assured because of his confidence in the Almighty to which all things are possible to him that believeth.

All of us remember the great soul stirring classic sermons of Henry Ward Beecher. You will recall that as a boy he was full of fear, and was bashful, shy, and retiring. His speech was very defective because of an enlarged and abnormal palate. He was given to constant prattle which was a subconscious compensation for his handicap. He believed that he would become a great preacher. He became what he believed he would be—the famous preacher of Plymouth Church. Discouragement seldom depresses the man whose focus is on the unfoldment of an ultimate desire. He who finds God within himself loses his misery and suffering.

The Greeks said that laughter is for the gods. Laughter is a medicine for many troubles. Man is the only being in the world who can laugh. Animals can't laugh. Laughter restores your perspective, takes your attention from yourself, and lets you think clearly and decisively. Make it a special point to laugh at your fears. Be sure to laugh when people irritate you, and by all means laugh at all the foolish, silly mistakes you made during the day. Laugh at yourself for being so stuffy and so serious. The greater the problem, the more humor you need. There is no self-pity nor self-condemnation where the laughter of God in the soul of man takes over.

I heard a boy the other day saying to his mother, "I laughed because I did not want to cry." The boy let the eggs and the milk fall on the street and instead of crying, he laughed. There is no use in crying over spilled milk.

Come back to the center within yourself where God abides. Here all is peace, bliss, harmony, and joy. Here you live beyond time and space. You are alone with God. You are in the sacred center of God's Eternal Love. On this rock you stand. You are impervious and invulnerable, and all the negation of the world cannot touch you. God by his very nature is for you, so who can be against you? There is no power in all the world to withhold from you success, achievement, and the realization of your heart's desire because *one with God is a majority.*

11

The Master Key to Harmonious Human Relations

Judge not, that ye be not judged. For with what judgment ye judge, ye shall be judged: and with what measure ye mete, it shall be measured to you again. And why beholdest thou the mote that is in thy brother's eye, but considerest not the beam that is in thine own eye? Or how wilt thou say to thy brother, Let me pull out the mote out of thine eye; and, behold, a beam is in thine own eye? Thou hypocrite, first cast out the beam out of thine own eye; and then shalt thou see clearly to cast out the mote out of thy brother's eye.

MATTHEW 7:1–5.

The master key to happy relationship with people is the application of the Golden Rule and in discovering that there is no one to change but yourself. As you would that men should think about you, think you about them in like manner. As you would that men should feel about you, feel you also about them in like manner. As you would want men to act toward you, act you toward them in like manner.

A study of the above mentioned verses and the application of the inner truths therein contained would transform our entire life. These verses teach the emancipation of man and reveal to him the solution to his individual as well as world problems.

We are told to *judge not that ye be not judged.* To judge is to think, to arrive at a mental verdict or conclusion in your mind. For example, I had a conversation with a man about fifty years old who had lost his position, and his financial situation had gone from bad to worse. He was extremely critical of the management in his former place of employment; he had a deep grudge against them. I explained to him that his negative, resentful attitude was highly destructive to him, that his hatred, resentment, and hostility were mental poisons which were robbing him of vitality, enthusiasm, strength, guidance, and peace of mind.

He began to see that the suggestion we give to another we give to ourselves because our mind is the creative medium. Therefore we actually create what we think and feel about the other. This is why the Bible says, *For with what judgment ye judge, ye shall be judged.* He ceased thinking negatively of his employers and sincerely wished for them health, happiness, and peace. He began to claim as follows: "God opens up a new door of expression for me. I am divinely guided every step of the way, and I follow the lead which comes to me. I sincerely wish for every man what I wish for myself." He found a new position, and is now on the way to the fulfillment of his dreams.

The good we do for others comes back to us in like measure; and the evil we do returns to us by the law of our own mind. If a man cheats and deceives another, he is actually cheating and deceiving himself. His sense of guilt and mood of loss will return to him some way, some time. His subconscious mind is a recording machine that faithfully reproduces what is impressed upon it. We cannot escape the law of our mind. Reward and retribution are reactions of our own mind based upon the way we directed our meditation. Our subconscious mind is impersonal and unchanging, neither considering persons nor respecting religious affiliations or institutions of any kind. It is neither compassionate nor vindictive. The way we think, feel, and act toward others returns at last upon ourselves.

Ask yourself now, "How am I behaving internally toward this other fellow?" This interior attitude is what counts. A woman wrote me about her husband, saying that he goes into a rage when he reads what certain newspaper columnists write in the newspaper. He came to see me, and I expatiated on the way our mind works and how emotionally immature it was to get angry because others write things with which we disapprove or disagree. My explanation to him was more or less along the following lines:

"Begin now to observe yourself; observe your reactions to people, conditions, and circumstances. How do you respond to the events and news of the day? It makes no difference if all the other people were wrong and you alone were right. If the news disturbs you, it is your evil, because your bad mood affected and robbed you of peace and harmony. You do not have to react negatively to the news or the comments of the broadcaster. You can remain unmoved, undisturbed, and poised, realizing he has a right to his expression and beliefs. It is never what a person says or does that affects us; it is our reaction to what is said or done that matters."

This explanation was the cure for this man, and he realized that with a little practice he could master his morning tantrums. His wife told me subsequently that he laughed at himself and also at what the columnists say. They no longer have power to disturb, annoy, and irritate him. He knew that he had been irritating himself in the past and blaming others for his discomfiture.

If all the people in the office or factory annoy you, isn't it a possibility that the vibration, annoyance, and turmoil may be due to some subconscious pattern or mental projection from you? We know that a dog will react ferociously if you hate or fear dogs. Animals pick up our subconscious vibrations and react accordingly. Many undisciplined human beings are just as sensitive as dogs, cats, and other animals.

A private secretary was very bitter toward some of the girls in her office because they were gossiping about her, and as she said, spreading vicious lies about her. She admitted that she did not like women. She said, "I hate women, but I like men." I discovered also that she spoke to the girls who were under her in the office in a very haughty, imperious, irritable tone. She pointed out that they took a delight in making things difficult for her. There was a certain pomposity in her way of speaking, and I could see where her tone of voice would affect some people unpleasantly.

I suggested a process of prayer, explaining to her that when she began to identify herself with spiritual values and commenced to affirm the Truths of life, her voice, mannerisms, and hatred of women would completely disappear. She was surprised to know that the emotion of hatred shows up in speech, actions, in our writings, and in all phases of our life. She ceased reacting in the typical, resentful, and angry way. She established a pattern of prayer which she practiced regularly, systematically, and conscientiously in the office.

The prayer was as follows: "The Infinite One thinks, speaks, and acts through me now; this is my real self. I now radiate love, peace, tolerance, and kindliness to all the girls who criticized and gossiped about me. I salute the Divinity in them. God speaks through me as peace, harmony, and love. Whenever I discover that I am about to react negatively, I say firmly, 'This is not the Infinite One speaking or acting.' Divine Love, Light, and Truth flow through me now."

The practice of this prayer transformed her life, and she found that all criticism and annoyance ceased. The girls became co-workers and friends along life's journey. She discovered that *there is no one to change but myself.*

Do you observe your inner speech? For example, you may be polite and courteous to the boss in the office, but when his back is turned, you are very critical and resentful toward him in your mind.

One day a salesman came to see me and described his difficulties in working with the sales manager of his organization. He had been with the company ten years and had received no promotion or recognition of any kind. He showed me his sales figures which were greater proportionately than the other men in the territory. He said that the sales manager did not like him, that he was unjustly treated, and that at conferences the manager was rude to him and at times ridiculed his suggestions.

I explained that undoubtedly the cause was to a great degree within himself, and that his concept and belief about his superior bore witness to the reaction of this man—*the measure we mete, shall be measured to us again.* His measure or concept of the manager was that he was mean, cantankerous, and he was filled with bitterness and hostility toward him. On his way to work he conducted a vigorous conversation with himself, filled with criticism, mental arguments, recriminations, and denunciations of his sales managers.

Whatever we give out mentally, we are inevitably bound to get back. This man realized that his inner speech was highly destructive, because the intensity and force of his silent thoughts and emotions and personally conducted mental condemnation and vilification of the sales manager entered into his own subconscious mind, bringing about the negative response from his boss, as well as creating many other physical and emotional disorders.

He began to pray as follows: "I am the only thinker in my universe. I refuse to give power to any person, place, or thing to annoy me or disturb me. I am responsible for the way I think about my boss. I know that God indwells him. I salute the Divinity in him. He is a spiritual being, living in God's universe, and he is governed over by God. I see him as God sees him. He is full of God's love, light, and truth. Whenever I think of him I say to myself, 'What is true of God is true of you.'"

He repeated this prayer out loud slowly, quietly, and feelingly, knowing that his mind is the garden of God, and whatever he plants in the garden will come forth like seeds after their kind. He practiced mental imagery every night prior to sleep this way: He imagined that his sales manager was congratulating him on his fine work, on his zeal and enthusiasm, and wonderful response from customers. He felt the reality of all this, felt his handshake, heard the tone of his voice, saw him smile. He made a real mental movie, dramatizing it in his own way, according to the Golden Rule and the Law of Love. Night after night he conducted this mental movie, knowing that the subconscious mind was the receptive plate on which his conscious imagery would be impressed. Gradually by a process of what may be termed mental and spiritual osmosis, the impression was made on the subconscious, and the expression automatically came forth. The sales manager called him up to San Francisco, congratulated him, and gave him a new assignment as Division Sales

Manager over one hundred men with a big increase in salary. He changed his concept and estimate of his boss, and the latter responded accordingly.

Like attracts like; birds of a feather flock together. Is it not possible that your associate's crotchety, petulant, critical attitude is a reflection of your own inner frustrations and suppressed rage? What this person says or does cannot really hurt you, except you permit him to disturb you. The only way he can annoy you is through your own thought. For example, if you get angry, you have to go through four stages in your mind: You begin to think about what he said. You decide to get angry and generate a mood of rage. Then you decide to act; perhaps you talk back and react in kind. You see that the thought, emotion, reaction, and action all take place in your mind. When you become spiritually mature, you do not respond negatively to the criticisms and resentment of others. To do so would mean that you had descended to that low mental vibration and become one with the negative atmosphere of the other. Identify yourself with your aim in life and do not permit any person, place, or thing to deflect you from your sense of oneness with the Infinite One who thinks, speaks, and acts through you.

You have the faculty to enter into the Secret Place of the Most High and commune with God. Here you live beyond time and space. In this spiritual union with the Divine you have a sense of inner peace. You are one with God. You refuse to descend from this high level of awareness. Your inner peace and sense of oneness with the Infinite One is your impregnable fortress. You never surrender your inner poise and sense of inner peace. "One with God is a majority." "If God be for you, who can be against you?"

Freud said, "Unless the personality has love, it sickens and dies." Love is understanding, goodwill, and it is respecting the God in the other person. The more love and good will you radiate, the more comes back to you. If you puncture the other fellow's ego and wound his estimate of himself, you cannot gain his goodwill. Recognize that every man is an incarnation of the Almighty, and that he wants to be loved, appreciated, and important to the world. Recognize that the other is conscious of his true worth and that he feels the dignity of being a son of the Living God. As you do this consciously and knowingly, you build the other person up, and he returns your love and goodwill.

Begin to see sermons in stones, tongues in trees, songs in running brooks, and God in everything. Begin to see God in everybody, and you will find that God begins to shine through that other in all His pristine glory. You owe every man respect and love. You must respect the God in him and identify yourself with the Creative Love in him.

During a lecture series in Town Hall early this year for Dr. Raymond Barker, Minister of Religious Science, an actor told me that the audience booed and hissed him on his first appearance on the stage. He said the play was a bad one and that undoubtedly he did not play a good role. He pointed out that for months afterwards he hated audiences. He called them dopes, dummies, stupid, gullible, etc. He quit the stage in disgust and went to work in a drug store for a year. One day he entered Town Hall and heard Dr. Barker speak on "How to Get Along With Ourselves." That lecture changed his life. He went back to the stage and began to pray for the audience and for himself. He poured out love and goodwill, and every night he claimed that God's peace filled their souls, and that they were lifted up and inspired. For ten nights or more he claimed that God's peace filled his mind and that he was expressing himself at his highest level through the wisdom and intelligence of the Almighty. All during the performance he sent out love vibrations of God's grace to the audience. Today he is a great actor, and he loves and respects people. Your goodwill and esteem will be transmitted to others and be felt by them.

Information or news is constantly brought to your attention all day long through the medium of your five senses. You are the one who determines what your mental responses are going to be to the news conveyed. You can remain poised, serene, and calm, or you can fly into a rage, and as a result get an attack of migraine or experience some other form of pain.

The reason two men react differently to the same situation is based on the nature of their respective subconscious conditioning. Your personality is based on the sum total of all your opinions, beliefs, education, and early religious indoctrination. This inner attitude of mind conditions your response. One man will get angry when he hears a certain religious program, but his brother may enjoy it because one is prejudiced, and the other is not. Our subconscious convictions and assumptions dictate and control our conscious actions.

You can recondition your mind by identifying with the eternal verities. Begin now by filling your mind with concepts of peace, joy, love, good humor, happiness, and goodwill. Busy your mind with these ideas. As you do, they will sink into the subconscious level and become orchids in the garden of God.

There are difficult people in the world who are twisted and distorted mentally. They are malconditioned. Many are mental delinquents, argumentative, unco-operative, cantankerous, cynical, and sour on life. They are sick psychologically. You would not condemn a person who had tuberculosis. Many people have deformed and distorted minds, probably warped during childhood. Many have congenital deformities. No one, for example, hates a hunchback; there are many mental hunchbacks. You have compassion and understanding. To understand all is to forgive all.

The hateful, frustrated, distorted, and twisted personality is out of tune with the Infinite. He resents those who are peaceful, happy, and joyous. Usually he criticizes, condemns, and vilifies those who have been very good and kind to him. His attitude is this: "Why should they be so happy when I am so miserable?" He wants to drag them down to his own level. Misery loves company.

A girl told me that she hated another girl in her office, the reason being that she was prettier, happier, had wealth, and was engaged to the boss of the company where they worked. After the marriage had taken place, one day the crippled daughter (by a former marriage) of the woman whom she hated came into the office. The child put her arms around her mother and said, "Mommy, mommy, I love my new daddy! Look what he gave me!" She showed her mother a wonderful new toy.

She said to me, "My heart went out to that little girl, and I knew how happy she must feel, and I got a vision of how happy this woman was. All of a sudden

I felt love for that woman, and I went into the office and wished her all the happiness in the world, and I meant it."

In psychological circles today, this is called empathy, which simply means the imaginative projection of your consciousness into that of another. She projected her mentality into that of the other woman and began to think from her brain. She was thinking and feeling as the other woman, and also as the child, because she likewise had projected herself into the mind of the child. She was looking out from that vantage point on the child's mother.

If tempted to injure or think ill of another, project yourself into the mind of Moses and think from the standpoint of The Ten Commandments. If prone to be envious, jealous, or angry, project yourself into the mind of Jesus and think from that standpoint. The words will come like a melody of God, *Love ye one another.*

No matter what the problem is, or how acute it may be, or how difficult the person, there is in the final analysis no one to change but yourself! When you change yourself, your world and environment will change. Begin with number one—yourself!

Don't permit people to take advantage of you and gain their point by temper tantrums, crying jags, or so-called heart attacks. These people are dictators who try to enslave you and make you do their bidding. Be firm but kind, and refuse to yield. Appeasement never wins. Refuse to contribute to their delinquencies, selfishness, and possessiveness. Remember, do that which is right. You are here to fulfill your ideal and remain true to the eternal verities and spiritual values of life which are eternal.

Give no one in all the world the power to deflect you from your goal, your aim in life, which is to bring more and more of God's wisdom, truth, and beauty into this world. Remain true to your ideal. Know that God guides you and that right action is yours, and whatever contributes to your peace, happiness, and fulfillment must of necessity bless all men who walk this earth. The harmony of the part is the harmony of the whole, for the whole is in the part, and the part is in the whole. The other fellow is an incarnation of God. All that you owe him is Love, and Love is the fulfilling of the Law.

About the Author

A native of Ireland who resettled in America, Joseph Murphy, Ph.D., D.D. (1898–1981) was a prolific and widely admired New Thought minister and writer, best known for his metaphysical classic, *The Power of Your Subconscious Mind*, an international bestseller since it first appeared on the self-help scene in 1963. A popular speaker, Murphy lectured on both American coasts and in Europe, Asia, and South Africa. His many books and pamphlets on the auto-suggestive and metaphysical faculties of the human mind have entered multiple editions—some of the most poignant of which appear in this volume. Murphy is considered one of the pioneering voices of affirmative-thinking philosophy.

Printed in the USA
CPSIA information can be obtained
at www.ICGtesting.com
JSHW012032140824
68134JS00033B/3019